MARY NORDEN

# Embroidery with wool

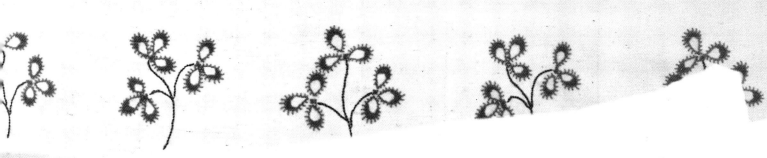

conran
OCTOPUS

Photography by SANDRA LANE

**This book is dedicated to my sisters: Catherine, Clare, Elizabeth and Monica**

First published in 1998 by Conran Octopus Limited,
37 Shelton Street, London WC2H 9HN

*Commissioning editor* **Suzannah Gough**
*Managing editor* **Helen Ridge**
*Copy editor* **Alison Bolus**

*Art editor* **Alison Barclay**

*Illustrator* **Carolyn Jenkins**
*Stylist* **Mary Norden**

*Production* **Julian Deeming**

A catalogue record for this book is
available from the British Library

ISBN 1 85029 930 7

PRINTED IN CHINA

# contents

Mention embroidery, and most people think of fabrics stitched with silky
cottons. Woollen threads, on the other hand, suggest knitting and tapestry.
But it was wool, rather than cotton, that was first used for embroidery.
Reaching the height of popularity in the seventeenth century, crewelwork, as
it was known, featured intricate and lavishly embroidered designs. In contrast,
but in keeping with my first embroidery book, Decorative Embroidery,
the designs I have created here are simple. They use crewel wool in a fresh
and, I hope, inspiring way, not just in the choice of patterns and stitches but
also in the colours and fabrics. So, as well as using linen, I have worked with
thick woollen blankets and throws, for example, to give some of the designs a
sensuous and tactile appeal. The designs, which are divided into four chapters —
Repeating Curls, Petals & Tendrils, Graphic Lines, Frippery — are inspired
by diverse and sometimes unlikely images, from the dried seedhead of
a poppy and ancient stone engravings to sea coral and an electric fan.
Whatever the inspiration, I hope you will find much to enjoy in this book.

repeating curls

# the influences for some of the designs in this chapter are obvious, almost conventional: the elegant paisley motif of an Indian shawl, for example, or the moon and stars of the midsummer night sky.

Other designs are inspired by subtler images: the curvaceous lines of sea coral or the ripples left by retreating waves on a sandy beach. But all these designs, whatever their inspiration, have a rhythm and a sense of movement. Even when the design is arranged formally, as with the repeating swirls on the purple throw, it still appears fluid.

# paisley curls

*Although we traditionally associate the paisley motif with the intricately patterned shawls of seventeenth- and eighteenth-century India, it was also popular for small-scale patterns known as foulards. The characteristic curling shape of the paisley motif was reduced like many other foulards to a regular geometric shape. These were printed on silk in neat, formal layouts for men's neckwear and dressing gowns. The paisley pattern used here for the curtain border and draw-string bag takes the main elements of the foulard print – the formality, the stylized motif, the simplicity of colour – but combines it with a boldness of scale for a modern interpretation.*

## MATERIALS

*For the curtain*
- DMC crewel wool in the following colours:
    cream – ecru
    blue 8799

(The amount of wool required depends on the length of the border to be worked. One skein of blue is sufficient to embroider three complete paisley shapes. One skein of cream will embroider as many as five paisleys.)
- plain purple linen fabric made up into the curtain style of your choice
- 7cm (3in) wide satin ribbon, enough to trim the embroidered edge of the curtain(s) – optional
- tracing paper

*For the draw-string bag*
- DMC crewel wool in cream – ecru (Two skeins are sufficient to work three paisley shapes.)
- 55cm (22in) of 90cm (36in) wide (or wider) coloured cotton or linen fabric
- approximately 150cm (60in) of thick cotton cord

*For both projects*
- dressmaker's carbon paper
- embroidery hoop
- crewel (embroidery) needle 5–7

## STITCHES USED

*For both projects*

| | |
|---|---|
| back stitch | blanket stitch |
| stem stitch | running stitch |

*For the curtain*

| | |
|---|---|
| chain stitch | French knot |
| lazy daisy stitch | |

For full details on stitches, see pages 128–37.

## TECHNIQUES

For full practical information on methods used in this project, refer to Techniques on pages 123–7.

## To work the curtain

Trace the template above with the tracing paper (the horizontal line is a guide, not part of the template). With a tape measure and pins, plan the placement of the paisleys along the curtain edge. To help keep the pattern in a straight line, draw a guideline (see page 124) 6cm (2½in) from the outer edge down the length of the curtain (this includes an allowance of 3.5cm/1½in for hemming). I rested each pair of paisleys on the guideline about 1cm (½in) apart. For a lighter pattern, position the paisleys further apart. Use dressmaker's carbon paper to transfer the pattern.

The entire design is worked with three strands of wool. Embroider the first paisley as follows: With blue, start at the curled tip of the paisley and work one tiny back stitch before changing to blanket stitch. As the tip widens, enlarge the stitches, extending their length to the second outline edge (see

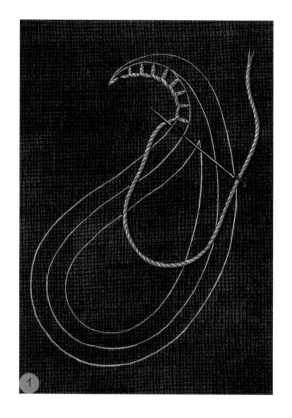

line round and back to where it first divides. Change to cream. Work a row of evenly spaced French knots between the lines of chain stitch. In the centre, work five groups of three lazy daisy stitches, one above the other (see illustration 2). Each group consists of two stitches that radiate out to the side, with the third placed centrally between the two. Follow the template markings for the correct lengths of each stitch.

Keep your work as neat as possible, because light shining through the curtain will highlight any loose threads. You may wish to line the curtain.

If you are embroidering a pair of curtains, reverse the pattern on one curtain so that both sets of paisleys match. To do this, turn the template over to give a mirror image. To create a symmetrical

*FAR LEFT: Working from left to right, embroider blanket stitch between the two outer lines of the paisley. The stitches should be evenly spaced and graduate to follow the curve of each paisley.*

illustration 1). Follow these two outline edges and stitch round and back to the tip, reducing the size of the stitches as the lines merge. Finish with a back stitch. Starting again at the tip of the paisley, work a line of stem stitch between the two rows of blanket stitch until the line divides. Follow the outline round and back to where it first divides. Embroider the inner outline edge in blue in stem stitch. Change to cream and work a row of running stitches between these two lines of stem stitch. In the centre of the paisley, work a row of back stitches and complete with five pairs of lazy daisy stitches, following the template for the correct length of each stitch.

For the second paisley: With blue wool, start at the curled tip and outline the motif in chain stitch. Starting again at the tip of the paisley and continuing in chain stitch, work a single line between the outline edges until the line divides. Follow the

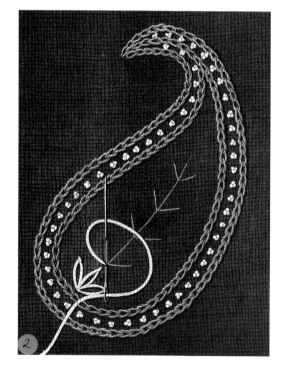

*LEFT: Work groups of lazy daisy stitch up the centre of the paisley. As the paisley lines narrow, slightly reduce the size of the angled stitches but keep the centre stitch of each group uniform in length.*

look, make sure that both of the curtains are embroidered on their inner, or leading, edge.

When the embroidery is complete, remove any tacking stitches. Hem, or if you want to trim your curtain with satin ribbon, fold the ribbon in half lengthwise and sew over the raw edge, taking in the 3.5cm (1½in) hem allowance.

**To work the draw-string bag**

Using a set square and a ruler, mark out a 46cm wide x 74cm long (18 x 29in) rectangle on the coloured linen or cotton fabric. Add on a 2.5cm (1in) seam allowance all round and cut out.

Enlarge the single paisley motif (right) to 245% on a photocopier. With dressmaker's carbon paper, transfer the pattern onto the fabric seven times by placing the first paisley 6cm (2½in) from the bottom edge (the longer side) of the rectangle and in the centre. Place three more paisleys on either side of this central one, 11cm (4½in) apart, measuring from the centre of one paisley to the next.

The entire design is worked with three strands of wool. Start at the curled tip of the paisley and work one small back stitch before changing to blanket stitch. As the tip widens, enlarge the stitches, extending their length to the second outline edge. Follow these two lines round and back to the tip, reducing the size of the stitches as the two lines merge. Starting again at the tip, embroider the inner outline edge in stem stitch. Outline all the petals, inside the paisley and around its outer edge, with stem stitch. In the middle of each central petal, work a line of running stitch (see photograph, far right). Finish with a line of stem stitch for the stem.

TEMPLATE

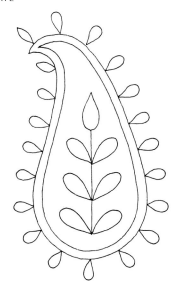

## To make up the draw-string bag

Using a sewing machine or small back stitches, join the two short edges of the embroidered rectangle (right sides together) to form a tube. Stop sewing 15cm (6in) from the top edge, leave a gap of 2.5cm (1in) through which to thread the cord, then continue sewing to the top.

For the base of the bag, cut out a circle of fabric 28cm (11in) in diameter – this includes a 2.5cm (1in) seam allowance. With right sides facing, pin and tack the circular base to the bottom of the bag, then stitch in place. Trim and press all the seams. Fold the top 7.5cm (3in) over to form a facing, and hem. Machine or hand sew a row of stitches on either side of the cord hole. These will form a cord casing and secure the facing into position. Thread the cord through the casing and cut to the desired length before knotting both ends together.

COLOUR GUIDE

Cream
ecru

Blue
8799

# coral lines

Like a meandering path, this design completely covers a cushion and a lampshade. Its inspiration could have come from a number of different sources: a child's scribbles, a snake's trail in the sand, even a garden maze. But for me the most obvious link is with coral. Although the looping and curling lines of coral are treated here in a very simple and bold way, their fragility is still apparent.

## MATERIALS

*For the turquoise cushion cover*

- DMC tapestry wool in turquoise 7036 (three skeins)
- DMC crewel wool in blue 8997 (four skeins)
- 1m (1yd) of 145cm (54in) wide plain turquoise cotton fabric (or less if not piping)

*For the cream cushion cover*

- DMC tapestry wool in cream – ecru (three skeins)
- DMC crewel wool in cream – ecru (four skeins)
- 1m (1yd) of 145cm (54in) wide plain cream cotton fabric (or less if not piping)

*For both cushion covers*

- crewel (embroidery) needle size 4–6
- 40cm (16in) zip
- 45cm (18in) cushion pad
- 2m (2yd) of piping cord (optional)

*For the lampshade*

- DMC crewel wool in the following colours:
  orange 8908 (two skeins)

red 8127 (two skeins)

- ready-made lampshade, 15cm (6in) high with a 25cm (10in) diameter bottom ring
- piece of lightweight orange cotton fabric, 60 x 40cm (24 x 16in)
- crewel (embroidery) needle size 6–8
- 1.2m (47in) of 2.5cm (1in) wide red binding tape
- 1.2m (47in) of coordinating trimming (optional)
- fabric adhesive

*For all projects*
- dressmaker's carbon paper
- embroidery hoop

## STITCHES USED
couching stitch
single laced running stitch
For full details on stitches, see pages 128–37.

## TECHNIQUES
For full practical information on methods used in this project, refer to Techniques on pages 123–7.

## To work the cushion cover (both colourways)
Using a set square and a ruler, mark out a 45cm (18in) square of fabric. Add on a 2.5cm (1in) seam allowance all round and cut out. Enlarge the template opposite to 45cm (18in) square on a photocopier and transfer to the fabric with dressmaker's carbon paper. Position it in the centre of the fabric.

The entire design is worked in couching stitch, using two strands of crewel wool to hold down the thicker tapestry wool. Always start the tapestry wool at the side edge, within the seam allowance. Do not cut off a length, but instead work directly with the skein, unravelling it as you sew. Follow each curling line across the cushion and back to the side seam. In this way there will be no visible joins of tapestry wool in the centre of the cushion and all ends can be secured in the seams during making up.

## To make up the cushion cover
Mark and cut out two pieces from the remaining fabric for each cover: one piece measuring 50 x 15cm (20 x 6in) and the other 50 x 40cm (20 x 16in). (These measurements include a 2.5cm/1in seam allowance all round.) To complete and to add piping, if desired, see page 126 for full instructions.

## To work the lampshade
Make a paper pattern of the lampshade (see page 127). Enlarge the template opposite until it is large enough to cover the pattern. Draw the outline of the lampshade pattern onto the template and transfer onto the fabric with dressmaker's carbon paper. To make working with an embroidery hoop easier, do not cut out the fabric until the stitching is completed.

**Turquoise
7036**

**Blue
8997**

**Cream
ecru**

**Orange
8908**

**Red
8127**

The entire design is worked in single laced running stitch using three strands of thread. First work running stitch in orange crewel wool along all the marked lines (the stitches and the spaces between them must be kept even); then lace with the contrasting red wool.

**To make up the lampshade**

Add a 2.5cm (1in) seam allowance all round the lampshade outline, then cut it out. Make up the shade (see page 127). Trim the top and bottom edges with coordinating braid, if desired. Once glued into position, hold in place with clothes pegs until dry.

# crescent moons

*The apparent spontaneity of this blue and white cushion cover belies the careful placement of each motif; had the motifs been positioned in a regular pattern, the design would have appeared rigid, even formal, while a too random approach would have resulted in an unbalanced and awkward pattern. To emphasize the strength of the design and add textural interest, I chose simple but dense stitching: the stars are so heavily embroidered with French knots that no fabric remains visible. In keeping with the nocturnal theme, the same motifs and stitches were used for a hot water bottle cover.*

**MATERIALS**

*For the cushion cover*

- DMC crewel wool in cream – ecru (eight skeins)
- 1.2m (4ft) of 90cm (36in) wide (or wider) blue linen or cotton fabric (or less if you are not adding piping)
- 46cm (18in) zip
- 55cm (22in) cushion pad
- 2.3m (90in) of piping cord (this is optional – see above)
- crewel (embroidery) needle size 5–7

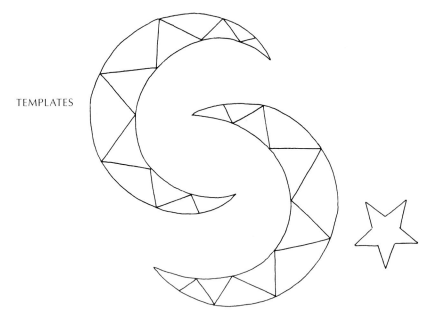

*For the hot water bottle cover*

- DMC tapestry wool in cream – ecru
  (Three skeins were sufficient for a cover
  with two moons and six stars.)
- coloured wool fabric to cover both sides
  of a hot water bottle (see page 25)
- cord or ribbon for tying neck of cover
- crewel (embroidery) needle size 2–4

*FAR RIGHT: After completing
the outline, embroider the
zig-zag line inside the
crescent in chain stitch,
working from right to left.*

*For both projects*

- tracing paper
- dressmaker's carbon paper
- embroidery hoop

### STITCHES USED

chain stitch

French knot

For full details on stitches, see pages 128–37.

### TECHNIQUES

For full practical information on methods used in
this project, refer to Techniques on pages 123–7.

**To work the cushion cover**

Using a set square and a ruler, mark out a 56cm
(22in) square on the fabric. Add on a 2.5cm (1in)
seam allowance all round and cut out.

Enlarge the template of the pair of crescents to
134%. Make eight copies. Cut out the copies very
roughly (to remove any excess paper) and space
them evenly over the square of fabric. Be careful
not to place the motifs too near the edge of the
fabric, otherwise they might get taken into the
seam allowance. To make sure that the design does
not end up looking too rigid and regular, alter
the angle of each pair of crescents so that they
are pointing in different directions. When you are
completely happy with the arrangement of the
crescents, pin them into position.

Now trace or photocopy the star motif 16 times
and scatter the cut-out copies over the fabric
between the moons. To create a denser pattern, add

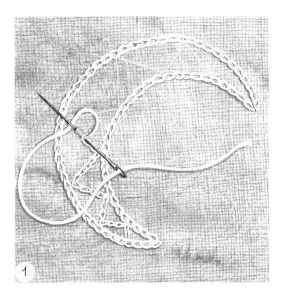

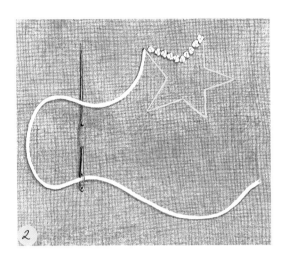

more stars. Once you are satisfied with your design, transfer all the templates onto the fabric using dressmaker's carbon paper.

The entire design is worked with three strands of wool. Work the crescent in chain stitch only. First embroider the outline and then the zig-zag line down the centre of the crescent, as indicated by the template markings (see illustration 1). Fill one side of the zig-zag pattern solidly with rows of chain stitch (see photograph, page 23). Work French knots for the stars; to maintain a good star shape, work the outline shape first (see illustration 2) and then fill the inside until no fabric is visible.

## To make up the cushion cover

For the backing fabric, you will need to mark and cut out two pieces of matching fabric, one measuring 15 x 61cm (6 x 24in) and the other 51 x 61cm (20 x 24in). (These measurements include a 2.5cm/1in seam allowance.) To complete and to add piping if desired, see page 126 for full instructions.

## To work the hot water bottle cover

First make a paper template of your hot water bottle. Simply lay the bottle flat on a piece of paper and, omitting the narrow neck and head for the moment, draw round the two sides and the base. Remember that the bottle will be larger when it is filled, so make your outline generous. Now extend the two side lines to above the top of the bottle by 5–10cm (2–4in). Square off the top. The resulting shape will now look like a rectangle with two curved corners. Using this template, mark out two hot water bottle shapes on the coloured wool fabric. Add a 2.5cm (1in) seam allowance all round, and cut out. Put one piece aside for the backing.

Enlarge both the crescent and star templates to the size of your choice on a photocopier. (Take several copies of the star so that you can plan your design before committing yourself.) When you are satisfied, transfer the design onto the fabric using dressmaker's carbon paper. Place the crescents nearer the curved bottom edge rather than the top edge, otherwise they will disappear into the folds of the neck when the fabric is gathered. Work the motifs as given above for the cushion cover.

## To make up the hot water bottle cover

Place the embroidered and backing fabric pieces right sides together, and, using a sewing machine or small back stitches, join along the two side edges and the curved base. Trim and press the seams. If the fabric is liable to fray, hem the top edge; then turn the cover right side out. Insert the water bottle and secure at the neck with a cord or ribbon (see photograph, page 22).

*FAR LEFT: Outline each star carefully with a continuous line of French knots. When the outline is complete, fill the star with French knots.*

COLOUR GUIDE

**Cream**
**ecru**

# reflecting swirls

*Curvaceous swirls, inspired by decorative wrought-iron railings, are embroidered along the edge of a luxurious throw made from the softest woollen fabric, which is in keeping with the sensuous look of the design. The swirls are embroidered in pairs so that they reflect each other, while on the lampshade they are simply laid on their sides and arranged singly around the bottom of the shade. I chose to use cable chain stitch for both projects. This stitch produces a raised, almost three-dimensional effect, and creates the illusion that actual lengths of fine chain have been carefully arranged in the shape of an 'S' on the surface of the fabric.*

## MATERIALS

*For the throw*

- DMC tapestry wool in cream – ecru. (Quantities required for the throw depend on the length of the border to be worked. One skein of cream wool is sufficient to embroider two double 'S' motifs.)

- coloured wool throw or blanket or, if you prefer to make your own, sufficient wool fabric

- cream cotton or silk fabric for backing (optional) to same size as the throw plus 2cm (¾in) all round for hemming allowance

- sufficient fringing to edge the length of the embroidered border (optional)

- crewel (embroidery) needle size 2–4

*For the lampshade*

- DMC crewel wool in cream – ecru (three skeins)

- ready-made lampshade, 15cm (6in) high with a 17cm (6¾in) base and a 10cm (4in) top

- piece of lightweight beige cotton fabric

- crewel (embroidery) needle size 5–7

- fabric adhesive

*For both projects*

- dressmaker's carbon paper

- embroidery hoop

## STITCHES USED

cable chain stitch

For full details on stitches, see pages 128–37.

## TECHNIQUES

For full practical information on methods used in this project, refer to Techniques on pages 123–7.

### To work the throw

Enlarge the double 'S' template to 164% on a photocopier. Using a tape measure and sewing pins, plan the placement of the design along one edge of your throw or piece of wool fabric. Mark a guideline (see page 124) 7.5cm (3in) from the bottom of the throw to help keep the motifs level. (This measurement includes a 2cm/³⁄₄in seam allowance for attaching the backing.) I positioned each of my double 'S' motifs 1cm (³⁄₈in) apart. Use dressmaker's carbon paper to transfer the pattern onto the fabric.

The entire border design is worked in cable chain stitch using tapestry wool.

### To make up the throw

When the embroidery is complete, remove any tacking stitches. Lay the piece of fringing along the right side of the embroidered border edge, so that the fringe lies on top of the fabric and the raw edges are together. Place the lining fabric on top of the throw and pin and tack the layers together all round. Machine stitch both sides and the fringed end, making a 2cm (³⁄₄in) seam, then turn the throw right side out. Press the seams. Turn under 2cm (³⁄₄in) on the remaining edge of both the throw and the lining, and slip stitch them together.

### To work the lampshade

First make a paper pattern or template of the lampshade (see page 127) and cut it out. Mark this shape on the fabric using a washable marker pen. Enlarge one of the 'S' shapes to 104% on a photocopier, then, with a ruler and pencil, plan the placement of the motifs on the shade, spacing them evenly and on their sides. Transfer the design using dressmaker's carbon paper. Because the pattern is so close to the lampshade outline, wait until you have finished stitching before cutting out the fabric.

The entire design is worked in cable chain stitch using three strands of crewel wool.

### To make up the lampshade

Add a 2.5cm (1in) seam allowance all round the lampshade outline, then cut it out. Make up the lampshade, referring to page 127.

COLOUR GUIDE

**Cream
ecru**

*repeating curls* ● 29

# sea waves

*We photographed this project on the south coast of England, on the beach where the idea for the design first came to me. A simple repeating pattern, it is made up of alternate straight and wavy lines, the former representing wooden breakwaters and the distant horizon, and the latter either waves or the undulating lines on the sand caused by the retreating tide. I deliberately chose colours to echo those of the shore – driftwood, sand and sea. I left a deep frayed border on the cushion, and as we took the photograph, the wind blew, making the border ripple and take on the shape of a wave.*

## MATERIALS

*For the cushion cover*
- DMC crewel wool in the following colours:
    beige 8505 (four skeins)
    pale blue 8209 (four skeins)
    blue 8208 (four skeins)
- 50cm (20in) of 90cm (36in) wide (or wider) cream linen fabric (If you want to fray the edges, choose a loosely woven linen.)

*For the tablecloth*
- DMC crewel wool in the following colours:
    beige 8505
    pale blue 8209
    blue 8208
    (Quantities for the tablecloth depend on the size of the cloth. For my 50cm/20in wide border running along one edge only, two skeins of each colour were sufficient.)
- a plain cotton or linen tablecloth or, if you wish to make your own, sufficient cotton or linen fabric made up as required

*For both projects*
- dressmaker's carbon paper
- embroidery hoop
- crewel (embroidery) needle size 4–6

## STITCHES USED

    guilloche stitch      French knot

    stem stitch          running stitch (cushion only)

For full details on stitches, see pages 128–37.

## TECHNIQUES

For full practical information on methods used in these projects, refer to Techniques on pages 123–7.

### To work the cushion cover

Using a set square and a ruler, mark and cut out two 45cm (18in) squares of linen fabric. Put one piece aside for the cushion backing. On the front piece, carefully mark out a guideline (see page 124), 5cm (2in) in all round, thus giving you an inner 35cm (14in) square. This is the actual cushion size.

    Enlarge the wave template to 35cm (14in) in length on a photocopier. With a measuring tape and pins, mark out the placement of the pattern. Repeat

COLOUR GUIDE

**Beige**       **Pale blue**       **Blue**
**8505**       **8209**       **8208**

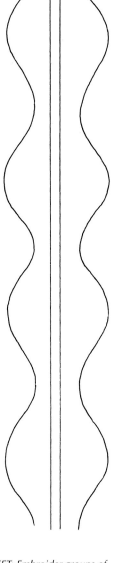

the wave design four times across the cushion cover, placing the centre of the first design 4cm (1¾in) from the cushion outline and the following designs 9cm (3½in) apart, always measuring from the centre of the design (i.e., between the two straight lines). Transfer the design using dressmaker's carbon paper.

The entire design is worked with three strands of wool. Work all the wavy lines in guilloche stitch as follows: With beige, embroider three satin stitches side by side to form small blocks at regular intervals (see illustration, right). The wavy line drawn on the fabric should run through the centre of each block (i.e., the middle stitch). Thread pale blue in and out of these blocks in both directions to form a chain-like effect of circles. Into the centre of each circle, embroider a French knot in blue. To finish, and with the same blue, stitch the straight lines in stem stitch.

## To make up the cushion cover

Place the embroidered cover squarely over the backing, wrong sides together. Following the border line, work a row of running stitch with three strands of beige wool round three sides of the cover. Insert the cushion pad and finish the fourth side with more running stitch. Fray the edges to the desired amount.

## To work the tablecloth

Enlarge the wave template to 232% on a photocopier. To help position the pattern so that it is completely level along the border of the tablecloth, mark a guideline (see page 124) 12cm (5in) in from the unhemmed border edge (this includes a hem allowance). In addition, mark the centre of the border edge. Transfer the motif onto the cloth with dressmaker's carbon paper so that one of the straight lines rests on the guideline.

To ensure that the border pattern finishes symmetrically at both side edges, work as follows: Position the wave motif so that its centre point corresponds to the centre of the border edge, and continue to repeat the waves on either side of this until you reach both side edges of the cloth. Repeat on the opposite end of the cloth.

The entire design is worked with three strands of crewel wool and is embroidered in the same way as the cushion cover.

*LEFT: Embroider groups of three satin stitches along the guideline, keeping the stitches and spacing even. It helps to work the middle stitch first on the line, followed by the two stitches on either side.*

petals & tendrils

# Much of design is about the paring down of shapes and lines, as well as colours, so that only the essentials remain. A few sinuous lines with the simplest of petal and leaf shapes are all that are needed to convey an exotic

trailing vine. The use of pale colours for the Wispy Tendrils project – pinks on cream linen – gives a sense of softness and femininity, which is in keeping with the delicate design. In sharp contrast, shades of blue, a traditional colour combination, were used for the Jacobean Blooms to emphasize the historical background of the design.

# jacobean blooms

*Towards the end of the seventeenth century, woollen embroidery, or Jacobean crewelwork as we now call it, was very fashionable. It decorated bed covers, valances, wall hangings and curtains with gracefully entwining branches and stems, curling leaves and exotic flowers. My Jacobean-style design, which I have placed on two cushions, is relatively simple. It uses a restricted colour palette characteristic of traditional crewelwork: shades of blue, ranging from a deep indigo to a soft grey-blue.*

## MATERIALS

*For the navy cushion cover*
- DMC crewel wool in the following colours:
  - cream – ecru (five skeins)
  - pale blue 8932 (five skeins)
- 1.1m (3ft 6in) of 90cm (36in) wide (or wider) denim blue linen (or less if not piping)

*For the cream cushion cover*
- DMC crewel wool in the following colours:
  - navy 8205 (five skeins)
  - mid blue 8208 (five skeins)
- 1.1m (3ft 6in) of 90cm (36in) wide (or wider) cream linen (or less if not piping)

*For both projects*
- 40cm (16in) zip for both cushions
- 45cm (18in) cushion pad for both cushions
- 2m (2¼yd) of piping cord (optional)
- dressmaker's carbon paper

- embroidery hoop
- crewel (embroidery) needle size 4–6

## STITCHES USED

| | |
|---|---|
| fly stitch | chain stitch |
| back stitch | lazy daisy stitch |
| stem stitch | satin stitch |

running stitch       double cross stitch

For full details on stitches, see pages 128–37.

## TECHNIQUES

For full practical information on methods used in this project, refer to Techniques on pages 123–7.

### To work the navy cushion cover

With a set square and ruler, mark out a 45cm (18in) square piece of fabric. Add on a 2.5cm (1in) seam allowance all round and cut out. Enlarge the template to 206% on a photocopier and transfer it onto the fabric using dressmaker's carbon paper. Make sure the template is placed in the centre.

The entire design is worked using three strands of wool. First work the main stem in fly stitch and cream. Start at the top, at the point where the stem

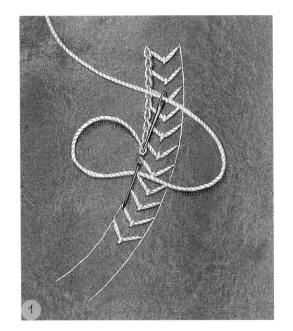

*LEFT: In each alternate flower segment, stitch rows of running stitch. Arrange them in lines radiating out from the centre.*

divides into two, and then continue down towards the base, enlarging the stitch as the stem widens. Keep the distance between each stitch even. On either side of these stitches and following the marked lines, work chain stitch (see illustration 1). Still working in chain stitch, complete all the stems and tendrils, using cream for the stems that support either leaves or flowers and blue for the three tendrils.

Next work the four larger leaves. With blue wool, embroider the centre vein of each leaf in back stitch. On either side of the veins, work a pair of lazy daisy stitches every second back stitch. These stitches should reduce in length as the leaf narrows. Change to cream wool to outline the leaves in chain stitch. Outline the remaining leaves in chain stitch and cream (except those at the base of each flower head). For any remaining leaf detail, work in stem stitch using blue wool.

Finally, work the three flowers. Start at the outer edge of each flower, embroidering a petal edge of

*FAR LEFT: After completing fly stitch down the centre of the main stem, work a line of chain stitch on either side, making sure the stitches cover the tips of each fly stitch.*

solid satin stitch in cream (see photograph, far left). The stitches should be close enough together so that no fabric is visible. Work the outer and dividing lines of each flower head in stem stitch, starting each line at the flower head base and finishing with the line merging into the satin stitch. Change to blue thread and complete as follows. Fill the two outer and centre flower head segments with lines of running stitch. Starting at the segment base, stitch radiating lines of running stitch, adding more lines as the segment widens (see illustration 2, page 41). Fill the two remaining segments with eight or nine scattered double cross stitches. To finish, at the base of each flower head work the pairs of small leaves in blue satin stitch, placing the stitches across the leaf shape.

## To work the cream cushion cover

Mark out your fabric square following the instructions given for the navy cover. Enlarge two leaves of your choice from the template to 227% on a photocopier. To help you plan the placement of your pattern, copy one leaf five times and the other leaf four times. Cut round these copies very roughly to remove excess paper. Lay the fabric square flat and arrange the leaves on it, being careful not to place them too near the edge of the fabric, as they might be taken up into the seam. To prevent the design from looking too rigid and regular, make sure you alter the angle of the leaves so that they are pointing in different directions (see photograph, above right). When you are completely satisfied with the arrangement, pin the copies temporarily to mark their position, then transfer the design onto the fabric using dressmaker's carbon paper.

The entire design is worked with three strands of wool. Both leaves are worked exactly as for the navy cushion, except in the choice of colours: the larger leaf is outlined in navy and detailed with mid blue; the colours are reversed for the smaller leaf.

## To make up both cushion covers

For the backing fabric you will need to mark and cut out two pieces of matching fabric, one piece 15 x 50cm (6 x 20in) and the other 40 x 50cm (16 x 20in). (These measurements include a 2.5cm/1in seam allowance all round.) To complete and to add piping around the edges, if desired, see page 126 for full instructions.

# indian sprigs

*I like the contrasts in this design: the delicate sprig motif is typical of a demure girl's dress, but the colours used – hot pink mixed with salmon orange and green – are vibrant and more in keeping with the colours of Indian saris. The outline of each flower petal is worked in blanket stitch with the stitches pointing outwards rather than inwards, so the flowers appear spiky, almost cactus-like, rather than typically smooth and rounded. I arranged the sprigs in rows but they could also be scattered randomly.*

## MATERIALS

*For the curtain*

- DMC crewel wool in the following colours:

    orange 8129 (two skeins)

    pink 8153 (two skeins)

    green 8401 (one skein)

    (These amounts are sufficient to embroider nine sprig motifs.)

- white or cream cotton or linen fabric, sufficient to make your own curtain, to the style of your choice

## To work the curtain

Enlarge the two sprig templates to 133% on a photo-copier. Using a tape measure and sewing pins, plan the placement of the flowers along the bottom of your curtain or fabric. Alternating the two different sprigs, I positioned each of my motifs at 12.5cm (5in) intervals, measuring from the base of one sprig stem to the next, and 6cm (2½in) from the bottom unhemmed edge of the curtain. For a denser border pattern, position the sprigs closer together. Use dress-maker's carbon paper to transfer the pattern.

The entire design is worked using two strands of crewel wool. Embroider satin stitch round the top edge of each flower petal, using the inner tip line as a guide for the length of the stitches. Work one of the flowers in orange and the other two in pink.

*FAR RIGHT: Beginning at the petal base, outline each petal in blanket stitch, increasing the length of the stitch as you work round to the petal tip. Decrease the length of each stitch as you return to the starting point. Keep the stitches evenly spaced.*

*For the tie-back*
- DMC crewel wool in the following colours:
  orange 8129 (one skein)
  pink 8153 (one skein)
  green 8401 (one skein)
- 65 x 26cm (25 x 10½in) of cotton or linen fabric (this includes a seam allowance)
- 1.4m (1½yd) of narrow tape for ties, cut into four

*For both projects*
- dressmaker's carbon paper
- embroidery hoop
- crewel (needle) size 6–8

### STITCHES USED

| satin stitch | blanket stitch |
|---|---|
| French knot | stem stitch |

For full details on stitches, see pages 128–37.

### TECHNIQUES

For full practical information on methods used in this project, see Techniques on pages 123–7.

Varying the arrangement of these two colours will prevent the sprigs from looking unnaturally identical (i.e., do not always stitch the petals of the flower in the centre of the sprig with orange). Use blanket stitch to outline each petal, working with orange for those petals tipped with pink and pink for those tipped with orange. Start at the petal base and enlarge the stitches slightly as you embroider round to the tip, then reduce them as you work back to the base (see illustration, below left).

Work three or four French knots in the centre of each flower and finally embroider the stems of each sprig with green in stem stitch.

It is important to keep your work as neat as possible, because light shining through the curtain will highlight any loose threads. Alternatively, you may wish to line the curtain.

**To work the tie-back**

On the tie-back fabric mark a guideline (see page 124) centrally along the fabric. Enlarge the two sprig templates to 133% on a photocopier. Using dress-maker's carbon paper, transfer the design onto the tie-back. Place six sprigs in a straight line along the length of the fabric, alternating the two different motifs as described above and using the guideline for positioning. I placed my sprigs 10cm (4in) apart, measuring from the base of one stem to the next. The design is worked exactly as for the curtain.

**To make up the tie-back**

Fold the embroidered tie-back fabric in half lengthwise, with right sides facing, and machine stitch along the long edge to form a tube. Turn right side out.

Press the fabric lightly, making sure that the line of flower sprigs is positioned along the middle of the tie-back and that the seam is lying on the reverse side. Tuck in the two side ends and, before stitching them closed, slip in approximately 1cm (½in) of the ends of the four tapes. Each tape should be positioned 2.5cm (1in) from the top or bottom edge on both ends of the tie-back. Stitch both ends closed. Stitch all round the tie-back very close to the edge to make it crisper and to keep the layers together.

COLOUR GUIDE

Orange
8129

Pink
8153

Green
8401

# autumn leaves

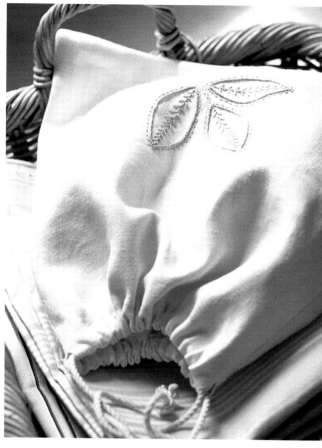

The most obvious way of altering the look or feel of a design is to enlarge or reduce its scale or to simplify the detailing. Different effects can also be achieved by using different stitches, or by changing the colour. All these devices have been used on the throw to create three contrasting designs with one motif: for example, the leaf embroidered in a solid dark brown line of stem stitch is much more pronounced than the leaf outlined in cream running stitch.

## MATERIALS

*For the throw*

- DMC crewel wool in the following colours:
    brown 8838
    cream – ecru
  (The amount of wool required depends on the size of the throw and how densely scattered you want the leaves to be. For my 112 x 155cm/44 x 61in throw with 15 leaves – seven of version 1, and four each of versions 2 and 3 – five skeins of brown and four of cream were required.)
- woollen throw or, if you prefer to make your own, sufficient wool fabric
- 7cm (2¾in) wide satin ribbon sufficient in length to trim two opposite ends of the throw

1

2

3

*For the draw-string bag*

- DMC crewel wool in yellow – 8305 (one skein)
- 80 x 40cm (32 x 16in) of linen or cotton fabric
- 1m (1yd) of cord for the neck
- safety pin

*For both projects*

- dressmaker's carbon paper
- embroidery hoop
- crewel (embroidery) needle size 4–6

## STITCHES USED

| | |
|---|---|
| stem stitch | fern stitch |
| running stitch | blanket stitch |

For full details on stitches, see pages 128–37.

## TECHNIQUES

For full practical information on the methods used to make this project, refer to Techniques on pages 123–7.

**To work the throw**

Enlarge the three leaf templates to 132% on a photocopier. Make several copies of each and cut round them roughly to remove the excess paper. Lay the throw flat on the floor and scatter the copies over it. When you are completely satisfied with the arrangement, pin the copies in place. Transfer the leaves onto their marked positions on the fabric using dressmaker's carbon paper.

The entire design is worked using three strands of crewel wool. Embroider the three different styles of leaf as follows:

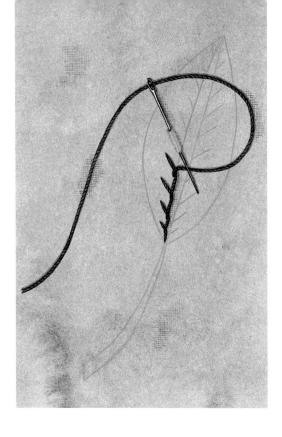

*LEFT: Starting at the leaf base and working from left to right, embroider blanket stitch up one side of the central leaf vein. Slant each stitch, and increase or decrease the length according to the template lines. Repeat on the other side of the leaf to complete the leaf veins.*

LEAF 1

With the brown wool, embroider two rows of slanting blanket stitch to create the veins of each leaf as follows: Start at the bottom of each leaf and, proceeding from left to right, work blanket stitch up the centre of the leaf towards the tip, slanting the angle of the stitches (see illustration, above). As the leaf widens, increase the length of each stitch, and then as the leaf narrows towards the tip, decrease the length of each stitch. Make sure you keep the stitches evenly spaced.

At the tip of the leaf, finish with one or two small back stitches, then turn and work down the other side of the central leaf vein in the same way. Outline the stem in stem stitch.

Change to the cream wool, and work two rows of running stitch to create the outline of each leaf, the outer line following the template line and the second line inside, but not quite touching (see photograph, page 52).

## LEAF 2

Using brown, work stem stitch for the outline of each leaf and for the leaf stem. Change to cream, and work a line of running stitch around the leaf outline, making sure the two rows are kept slightly separate. (This line is not marked on the template.) In the centre of each leaf, work two rows of running stitch, pairing the stitches.

## LEAF 3

Using cream, work stem stitch for the outline of each leaf. Change to brown, and work a line of running stitch around the leaf outline, making sure the two rows are kept slightly separate. (This line is not marked on the template.) Continue in running stitch to outline the leaf stem. Embroider a row of fern stitches down the centre of each leaf, keeping the stitches evenly spaced.

**To make up the throw**

Neatly hem the two longer side seams of the wool fabric. Fold the satin ribbon in half lengthwise and sew over the edge of the two remaining sides, encasing the unhemmed edges. At each end of the satin trim, tuck in the edges of the ribbon and stitch discreetly together.

**To work the draw-string bag**

Cut the fabric in half to make two 40cm (16in) squares. Enlarge the leaf template of your choice to 119% on a photocopier. Using dressmaker's carbon paper, transfer the design onto one of the squares of fabric. I positioned my motif 10cm (4in) from the bottom edge, measuring from the base of the stem, and with equal distances either side. This ensures the correct placement when the bag is made up.

The entire design is embroidered with three strands of crewel wool. Work the motif exactly as for Leaf 3 of the throw, but using yellow wool.

**To make up the draw-string bag**

With right sides facing, sew the back and front pieces together along the sides and bottom with 2cm (¾in) seams, leaving a 3cm (1⅛in) opening on both sides for the cord, approximately 2.5cm (1in) from the top. Turn under a 1cm (⅜in) hem along the top edge. Turn the bag to the right side and fold over the top to the inside so that the fold line falls mid-way along the openings. Stitch all round the top, 2.5cm (1in) down, to make a channel to hold the cord. The stitching line will pass about 1cm (⅜in) under the opening for the cord. Attach a safety pin to one end of the cord and use it to thread the cord through the channel; knot the ends together.

COLOUR GUIDE

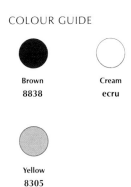

Brown
8838

Cream
ecru

Yellow
8305

# trailing flowers

*Embroidered over this cushion is a graceful design of trailing vines with flowers. Their sinuous lines cover the fabric completely yet retain an airy and delicate feel. Although the pattern is reminiscent of eighteenth- and nineteenth-century floral dress fabrics, it looks fresh and modern because of the colours used – cream on an almost glowing lime green linen. Textural interest is introduced by the different density of stitching within the petals and leaves. The solitary flowers featured on the buttons give a very different effect; without the flowing lines the design is no longer fluid.*

## MATERIALS

*For the cushion cover*

- DMC crewel wool in cream – ecru (12 skeins)
- 50cm (20in) of 115cm (45in) wide (or wider) coloured linen or cotton fabric (or less if not piping)

- 2m (2¼yd) of piping cord (optional)
- 40cm (16in) zip
- 45cm (18in) cushion pad
- crewel (embroidery) needle size 4–6

*For the button covers*
- DMC crewel wool in the following
  colours:
    lilac 8896
    blue 8798
    purple 8333
  (One skein of wool of each colour
  is more than enough for eight buttons.)
- small remnants of fine cotton or linen fabric
- button-covering kits – these may vary in size
  from 11–38mm (½–1½in) in diameter.
- crewel (embroidery) needle size 8–10

*For both projects*
- dressmaker's carbon paper
- embroidery hoop

*FAR RIGHT: Work all the template markings in chain stitch, starting with the leaf outline and working in towards the centre. The two inner lines can either be stitched as independent chains, following the template lines, or they can be tapered in towards the stem, as shown here. The direction of the stitching is optional.*

## STITCHES USED

| | |
|---|---|
| chain stitch | lazy daisy stitch |
| French knot | stem stitch |
| running stitch | |

For full details on stitches, see pages 128–37.

## TECHNIQUES

For full practical information on methods used in this project, refer to Techniques on pages 123–7.

### To work the cushion cover

With a set square and ruler, mark out a 45cm (18in) square piece of fabric. Add on a 2.5cm (1in) seam allowance all round and cut out. Enlarge the template to 45cm (18in) square on a photocopier and transfer it onto the fabric using dressmaker's carbon paper. Position it in the centre of the fabric.

The entire design is worked using three strands of wool. Work the five-petalled flowers first. Outline each petal with chain stitch, then fill the outlined petals with lazy daisy stitches. Work a dense cluster of French knots in the centre of each flower. For the remaining flowers, outline each petal with chain stitch before filling with more rows of chain stitch. Work a dense cluster of French knots in the centre.

For the leaves with side veins, first embroider the central vein and leaf stem in chain stitch before stitching the side veins in stem stitch. Complete each leaf with an outline of chain stitch. For the second style of leaf, work the outline first in chain stitch and then continue in towards the centre, working two more curved rows of chain stitch. Finish with one straight row in the centre (see illustration, above right). Embroider the remaining stems in chain stitch.

### To make up the cushion cover

For the backing fabric you will need to mark and cut out two pieces of fabric, one measuring 15 x 50cm (6 x 20in) and the other 40 x 50cm (16 x 20in). (These measurements include a 2.5cm/1in seam allowance all round.) To complete, and to add piping if desired, see page 126 for full instructions.

### To work the button covers

Enlarge or reduce the five-petalled flower head from the template, as necessary, to fit the buttons to be covered. With dressmaker's carbon paper, transfer the template several times onto your fabric, according to the number of covers you need. Leave a suitable gap between the motifs to allow for cutting out.

Stitch the flower heads as for the cushion, but with one strand of each wool and filling the petals with running stitch, rather than lazy daisy stitch.

When the button covers are complete, cut them out, leaving some excess fabric, and make up the buttons according to the kit instructions.

## COLOUR GUIDE

| | |
|---|---|
| **Cream**<br>**ecru** | **Lilac**<br>**8896** |

| | |
|---|---|
| **Blue**<br>**8798** | **Purple**<br>**8333** |

# wispy tendrils

*This delicate design, running along the edge of an old linen bed cover, has been pared down to a few essential lines; there are no leaves or flowers, just a few wispy tendrils reaching out from one main stem. The tendrils are so light and simple, they could have been sketched with a feather. Both the bed cover and the lampshade are embroidered in couching stitch. The thickness of yarn gives a raised, almost three-dimensional effect, as if the tendrils had been laid flat on the fabric.*

## MATERIALS

*For the bed cover*

- DMC tapestry wool in pink 7202
- DMC crewel wool in pale pink 8111 (Quantities of wool depend on the length of the border to be worked. For my 165cm/65in long bed cover, five skeins of the tapestry wool and four skeins of the crewel were required.)
- linen or cotton bed cover or, if you prefer to make your own, sufficient linen or cotton fabric made into a cover of the required size

*For the lampshade*

- DMC tapestry wool in cream – ecru (two skeins)
- DMC crewel wool in green 8420 (two skeins)
- a ready-made lampshade, measuring 21cm (8¼in) high with an 18cm (7in) base and a 9cm (3½in) top
- a piece of cotton fabric large enough to cover the lampshade
- fabric adhesive

*For both projects*

- dressmaker's carbon paper
- embroidery hoop
- crewel (embroidery) needle size 5–7

## STITCHES USED

couching with cross stitch

For full details on stitches, see pages 128–37.

## TECHNIQUES

For full practical information on methods used in this project, refer to Techniques on pages 123–7.

### To work the bed cover

Enlarge the template to 183% on a photocopier. Using dressmaker's carbon paper, transfer the template onto your bed cover as instructed below.

To help position the pattern in a straight line along the cover border, mark a guideline (see page 124) 18cm (7in) from the hemmed edge of the fabric. Working from the left side edge to the opposite right edge, position the main stem so that it begins and ends on the guideline. Continue to repeat the pattern until it runs along the whole length of the cover. Match the end of one template with the beginning of the next to give a continuous pattern.

Start stitching, working from right to left. Bring the pink tapestry wool up through the fabric at the right-hand end of the main stem. Following the line of the main stem, hold the thread down with small crosses using three strands of crewel wool. When the main stem is completed along the whole length of the cover, work the shorter tendrils in the same way. At the end of each tendril, take both the tapestry and crewel wools through to the back of the work and fasten them off before starting the next tendril. It is important not to carry any yarn across the back of the fabric because long strands are very likely to get caught, thus damaging the embroidery.

## To work the lampshade

First mark both the top and bottom rim of the shade into four equal parts, as though cutting a cake, with a marker pen. These are the guide points for the placement of the four rows of pattern. Make a paper pattern or template of the shade (see page 127), starting at an equal distance between two of these markers. This is to make sure the seam line falls exactly between two pattern lines. As you roll the frame across the paper in an arc, mark the corresponding positions of the guide points onto the paper. Draw the outline of the lampshade template and the guide points onto the fabric. To make working with an embroidery hoop easier, do not cut out the fabric until the embroidery is finished.

Enlarge the template to 186% on a photocopier, and transfer the pattern onto the fabric using dressmaker's carbon paper. Starting at the bottom of the shade, place as much of the pattern as possible (this depends on the size of the shade) vertically up the height of the shade in line with the guide points. I used four tendrils on my lampshade, each starting at one of the bottom guide points.

Stitch as for the bed cover, keeping the back of the work as neat as possible, because when the lamp is on, any stray threads will be visible.

## To make up the lampshade

Add a 2.5cm (1in) seam allowance all round the lampshade outline, then cut it out. Make up the lampshade, referring to page 127. Trim the top and bottom edges of the lampshade with coordinating braid if desired. Once this is glued into position, hold the braid in place with clothes pegs until dry.

TEMPLATE

COLOUR GUIDE

Pink
7202

Pale pink
8111

Cream
ecru

Green
8420

graphic lines

# in contrast to the fluid patterns in Repeating Curls, the other geometric-style chapter, these designs are more formal. Circles and straight lines are used like building blocks to create strong, geometric motifs that can

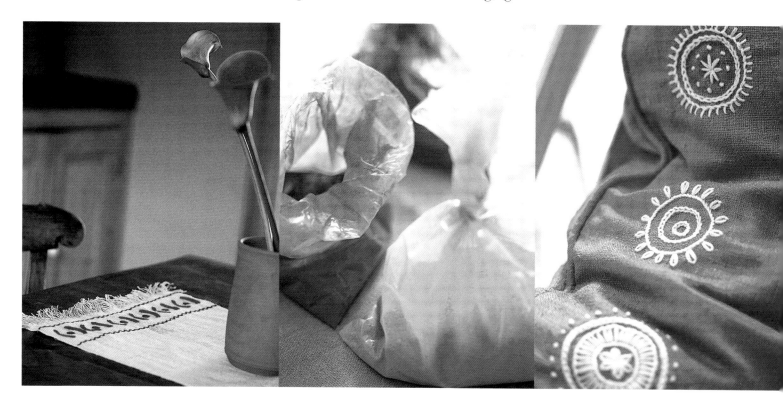

be arranged in lines or grids to create all-over or border patterns. Some of the motifs are familiar but given a contemporary slant: the classic combination of noughts and crosses is invigorated by playing with the scale of each motif, while a spiral and pinwheel pattern is made even simpler by its cream-on-cream stitching.

# spirals & pinwheels

The discreet embroidered pattern on this luxurious cream blanket belies the original inspiration: an electric fan, whirling away on a hot summer's day. Stylized and simplified into a classic pinwheel motif, the pattern is made up of a set of lines radiating from a central point, with each line curved as if bent by the wind. Wishing to alternate this motif with another, yet retain the sense of movement, I chose the spiral. This graphic shape consists of one continuous and circling line that looks as if it is either spreading outwards or contracting inwards like a whirlpool. The two motifs are arranged in a line along the edge of the blanket and stitched in cream, so the emphasis is placed on the texture of the stitches, rather than on the colour. In contrast, and on a much smaller scale, the motifs are stitched in cream on orange buttons which, when grouped together, look more like tiny iced cakes.

**MATERIALS**

*For the blanket*

- DMC tapestry wool in cream – ecru
  (One skein is plenty for two motifs.)
- wool blanket or suitable wool fabric (a blanket or fabric that is smooth, with a felt-like appearance rather than fluffy, is ideal)
- length of 7.5cm (3in) wide satin ribbon, 5cm (2in) longer than the embroidered edge
- crewel (embroidery) needle size 2–4

*For the button covers*

- DMC crewel wool in the following colours:
  cream – ecru
  red 8127
  (One skein of each colour is more than enough for six buttons.)
- small pieces of orange cotton or linen fabric

- button-covering kit, 38mm (1½in) in diameter
- crewel (embroidery) needle size 6–8

*For both projects*
- dressmaker's carbon paper
- embroidery hoop

## STITCHES USED

chain stitch

French knot

For full details on stitches, see pages 128–37.

## TECHNIQUES

For full practical information on methods used in this project, refer to Techniques on pages 123–7.

### To work the blanket

Enlarge the two motifs to 113% on a photocopier. Using a tape measure and sewing pins, plan the placement of the alternating pinwheels and spirals along the top edge of your blanket or fabric. Mark a guideline (see page 124) 10cm (4in) from the unhemmed edge. Position the motifs 12.5cm (5in) apart from each other, always measuring from the centre of one motif to the next, with their centres on the guideline. When you are satisfied with the arrangement, transfer the pinwheels and spirals onto the fabric using dressmaker's carbon paper.

The entire design is worked using one strand of tapestry wool. Each spiral is worked in chain stitch only. You can start either from the centre of each spiral working out or from the end of the spiral working in. Either way, once the stitching of a spiral has started, it must continue in the same direction.

Each pinwheel is worked in French knots only. Starting at the centre and following the marked lines, embroider the stitches close together, but make sure that there is a slight gap between each one (see illustration, above).

When the border is complete, trim the top of the blanket with ribbon (see Autumn Leaves, page 53).

### To work the button covers

Reduce the two templates to 48% on a photocopier and transfer them onto the fabric using dressmaker's carbon paper. Transfer as many times as the number of covers required. Be careful not to place the motifs too close together to allow for cutting out.

Each design is worked with three strands of wool. Work the spirals as given above for the blanket. The pinwheels are worked in two ways. The first uses French knots, as in the blanket border, while the second is worked in chain stitch and then finished with four or five French knots in contrasting red thread in the centre. When the embroidered covers are complete, cut them out, leaving some excess fabric, and make up the button covers according to the instructions supplied with the kit.

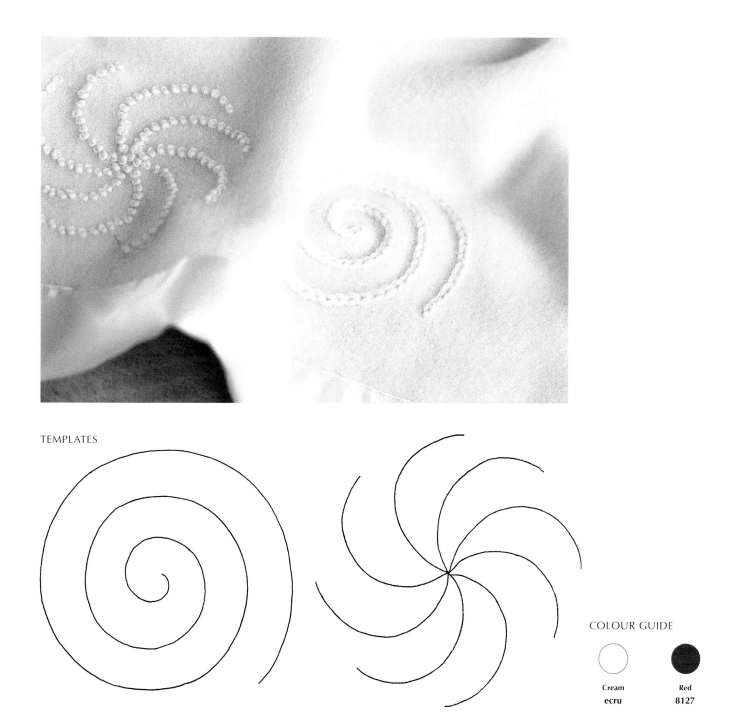

TEMPLATES

COLOUR GUIDE

Cream
**ecru**

Red
**8127**

# noughts & crosses

*In a style reminiscent of woven Navajo blankets or painted African pots, this wonderfully simple pattern, consisting of no more than a cross and a circle, is worked across a thick wool cushion cover and along the edge of a fringed throw. The scale of the circle has been chosen carefully to complement the stitch used – eyelet buttonhole – and the thickness of the wool. Any larger, and the length of the stitching would be impractical.*

## MATERIALS

*For the throw*

- DMC tapestry wool in the following colours:

  green 7540

  beige 7423

  (Quantities for the throw depend on the length of the border to be worked. One skein of green wool is sufficient to embroider three crosses, and one skein of beige will embroider as many as eight noughts.)

- wool blanket or, if you prefer to make your own, suitable wool fabric (choose a fabric that is smooth rather than fluffy and has a felt-like appearance)

TEMPLATE

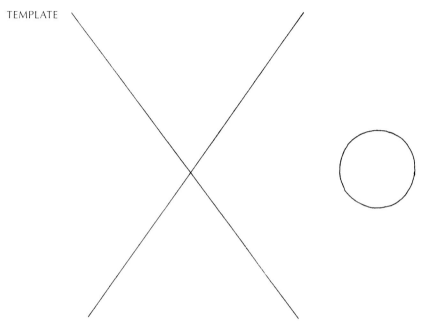

*For the cushion cover*
- DMC tapestry wool in the following colours:
  red 7108 (eight skeins)
  beige 7423 (one skein)
- 70cm (27½in) of 137cm (54in) wide plain wool fabric (as for the throw)
- a 65cm (26in) square cushion pad

*For both projects*
- dressmaker's carbon paper
- embroidery hoop
- crewel (embroidery) needle size 1–2

**STITCHES USED**

Pekinese stitch          eyelet buttonhole stitch
running stitch

For full details on stitches, see pages 128–37.

**TECHNIQUES**

For full practical information on methods used in this project, refer to Techniques on pages 123–7.

**To work the throw**

Enlarge the nought and cross template to 117% on a photocopier. Using a tape measure and pins, plan the placement of the pattern. To help position the motifs so that they are all level, mark a guideline (see page 124) 12cm (5in) from the bottom raw edge of the fabric. The noughts and crosses should be centred on this guideline. Transfer the motifs onto the border with dressmaker's carbon paper.

The crosses are embroidered in Pekinese stitch only. At the point where the second line crosses the first, simply stitch over the top of the first line. Work the noughts in eyelet buttonhole stitch, making sure the stitches are evenly spaced.

If you want a fringed edge to the throw, use sharp scissors to snip lengths of 5cm (2in) approximately 1cm (⅜in) apart. This is suitable only for felted wool fabric that does not fray. Should you wish to trim your throw with satin ribbon instead, refer to Autumn Leaves, page 53, for instructions.

**To work the cushion cover**

Mark and cut out two 68cm (27in) squares from the wool fabric. Put one square aside for the cushion backing. Using a tape measure and pins, plan the placement of the pattern as follows: First mark a 6cm (2½in) border all round with tailor's chalk or a washable fabric marker pen (see under Drawing a guideline, page 124), thus making an inner 56cm (22in) square. Inside this square, mark four guidelines for your four rows of noughts and crosses. Place the first line 5.5cm (2in) away from one inside square edge and then, moving across the cushion to the other side, place the following lines 15cm (6in) apart. The fourth line, as with the first, should be 5.5cm (2in) away from the opposite side.

Enlarge the nought and cross template to 117% on a photocopier. Transfer the motifs onto the fabric with dressmaker's carbon paper, using the guide-lines for placement, so that each nought and cross sits astride the line. Start the top of each row with a nought, positioning it 2cm (1in) away from the top edge of the inside square, then place a cross 6.5cm (2½in) away from the nought, measuring from the centre of one motif to the next. Repeat this pattern along the length of the cushion, always measuring from the centre of each motif. To embroider the pattern, follow the instructions given for the throw.

## To make up the cushion cover

Place the embroidered cushion front squarely over the backing piece, with wrong sides together, and stitch a row of running stitches in beige wool along the border line. Work three sides, then insert the cushion pad before completing the fourth.

If you wish, you could fringe the cushion cover as for the throw, provided you use a felted wool fabric that does not fray.

COLOUR GUIDE

**Red**
**7108**

**Green**
**7540**

**Beige**
**7423**

# contemporary circles

*Plants are a constant and rewarding source of inspiration. Look into the centre of a flower, perhaps a marigold or a peony, and you will see an orderly maze of petals and stamens arranged in radiating lines and circles. Such an organic pattern, when simplified and translated into an embroidery design, creates a strong contemporary motif which can be adapted in many ways. Simply by altering the spacing between the radiating lines or by working the circles as broken lines, numerous variations based on one image can be achieved.*

## MATERIALS

*For the curtain*

- DMC crewel wool in yellow 8725
  (The amount of wool required depends on
  the length of the curtain border to be
  embroidered. Five skeins were sufficient
  to work 13 circle motifs.)

- plain cream linen fabric, sufficient to make
  your own curtain

*For the cushion cover*

- DMC crewel wool in cream – ecru (six skeins)
- 1m (1yd) of 145cm (54in) wide plain
  coloured linen (or less if not piping)
- 40cm (16in) zip
- 50cm (20in) cushion pad
- 2.5m (1½yd) of piping cord (optional)

*For both projects*

- tracing paper
- dressmaker's carbon paper
- embroidery hoop
- crewel (embroidery) needle size 5–7

## STITCHES USED

French knot          chain stitch

12cm (5in) away from the unhemmed edge, again measuring from the centre of each circle. If you would prefer a denser pattern, position the circles closer together. Transfer the design onto the fabric using dressmaker's carbon paper.

The entire curtain border is worked using three strands of crewel wool.

## CIRCLE 1

Starting from the outside and working in, embroider a circle of French knots, followed by a circle of chain stitch. Between the next two circular outlines, work blanket stitch (see illustration 1) before edging the blanket stitches with a circle of stem stitch. For the star in the centre of the circle, embroider six radiating lazy daisy stitches; these should all emerge from one central point.

*FAR RIGHT: As you work out from the centre of the circle in blanket stitch, radiate the stitches slightly to follow the next circular outline.*

| | |
|---|---|
| blanket stitch | stem stitch |
| lazy daisy stitch | straight stitch |

For full details on stitches, see pages 128–37.

### TECHNIQUES

For full practical information on methods used in this project, refer to Techniques on pages 123–7.

### To work the curtain

Trace the three circle templates with the tracing paper. Using a tape measure and sewing pins, plan the placement of the circles along the edge of the curtain, alternating the three different designs (see photograph, page 78). I positioned each of my circles 10cm (4in) apart from each other, measuring from the centre of one to the centre of the next, and

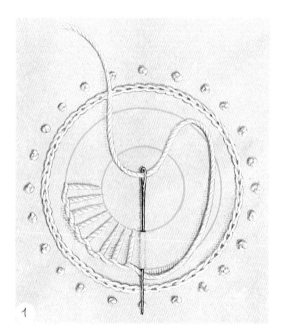

1

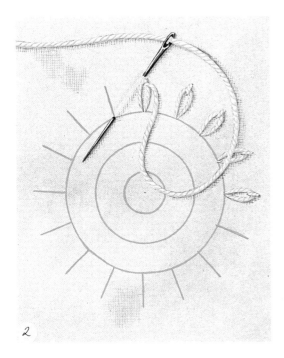

2

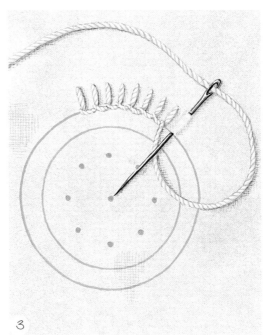

3

FAR LEFT: *For each radiating line of the circle, work a lazy daisy stitch. When each line is complete, bring the needle out again at the base of the next line.*

LEFT: *Working from left to right, outline the circle in reversed blanket stitch. Make sure the stitches are the same length and evenly spaced.*

## CIRCLE 2

Starting from the outside and working in, embroider lazy daisy stitch for each radiating line (see illustration 2) before working a circle of stem stitch. Work the two remaining circles in chain stitch.

## CIRCLE 3

Starting from the outside of the motif and working in, embroider a circle of reversed blanket stitch (see illustration 3). Inside this, work a circle of chain stitch, followed by a circle of eight French knots. For the star in the centre of the circle, embroider eight radiating straight stitches, all emerging from one central point.

It is important to keep your work as neat as possible, because light shining through the window onto the curtain will highlight any loose threads. Alternatively, you may wish to line the curtain.

### To work the cushion cover

With a set square and a ruler, mark out a 53cm (21in) square of coloured fabric. Add a 2.5cm (1in) seam allowance all round and cut out. Trace the three circle motifs with tracing paper. With a tape measure and sewing pins, mark out the arrangement of the pattern. All the circles are spaced 13cm (5in) apart (from centre to centre) and arranged in four rows, each with four circles. The outer circles are positioned 10cm (4in) in from the cover edge. Every alternate circle is design 2; the remaining circles are designs 1 and 3 placed randomly (see photograph, above far left).

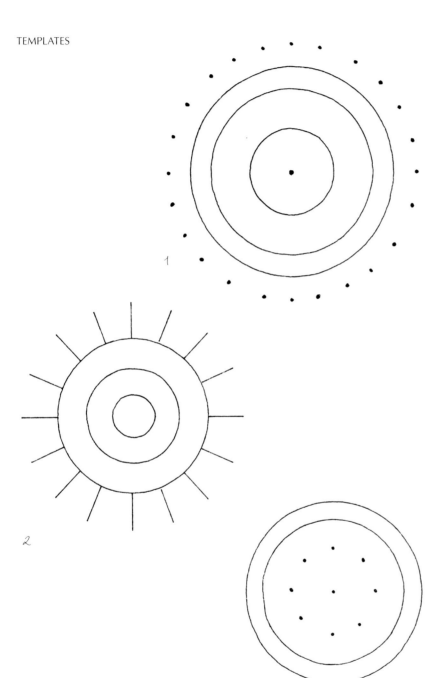

The entire design is worked using three strands of crewel wool. Embroider each circle motif as given for the curtain.

**To make up the cushion cover**

For the cushion back, you will need to mark and cut out two pieces of fabric, one measuring 15 x 58cm (6 x 23in) and the other 48 x 58cm (19 x 23in). To complete the cushion cover and add piping if desired, see page 126 for full instructions.

COLOUR GUIDE

**Cream
ecru**

**Yellow
8725**

# stars & stripes

This design combines woven stripes, embroidered crosses and colours in a graphic style that brings to mind Swedish fabrics from the 1950s. Using straight stitch as its basis, two different crosses are made, their size and spacing dictated by the width of the fabric stripe. Each cross is secured in the centre with one small straight stitch in a contrasting colour. This has a practical as well as decorative purpose; too long a thread on the surface of the fabric can easily get caught and pulled, thus distorting the fabric. Both the cushion cover and the lampshade are ideal projects for the beginner, as the stripes form a clear guide for working the stitches.

## MATERIALS

*For the cushion cover*

- DMC crewel wool in the following colours:
    yellow 8325 (eight skeins)
    plum red 8106 (three skeins)

- 70cm (27in) of 137cm (54in) wide (or wider) striped cotton fabric. (I chose a red, orange and cream striped fabric. The cream stripes – the area to be embroidered – were 2.5cm/1in wide; these alternated with 2cm/¾in red-coloured stripes.)
- 50cm (20in) of 90cm (36in) wide (or wider) cream fabric to make the cushion piping (optional)
- 2.5m (8ft) of piping cord (optional)
- 60cm (23in) cushion pad
- 50cm (20in) zip

*For the lampshade*
- DMC crewel wool in the following colours:
  green 8305 (three skeins)
  madder red 8221 (one skein)
- ready-made, straight drum lampshade, measuring 25cm (10in) high with a 10cm (4in) diameter
- 50cm (18in) x 30cm (12in) of striped cotton fabric
- 80cm (31in) of 1.5cm (½in) cream cotton tape for finishing
- fabric adhesive

*For both projects*
- embroidery hoop
- crewel (embroidery) needle size 4–6

## STITCHES USED
straight stitch
cross stitch

For full details on stitches, see pages 128–37.

## TECHNIQUES
For full practical information on methods used in the making of this project, refer to Techniques on pages 123–7.

### To work the cushion cover
Using a set square and a ruler, mark out a 58cm (23in) square on your fabric (this measurement may differ slightly depending on the width of the stripes). Make sure that the stripes are arranged symmetrically across the square (i.e., if one side of the square starts with a coloured stripe, the opposite side must

finish with one, too). Add on a 2.5cm (1in) seam allowance all round and cut out. Next work out the arrangement of the pattern. With a washable fabric marker pen and ruler, mark out the centre of each cross as follows: For the stripes with smaller crosses, place the first dot 3.5cm (1¼in) from the top raw edge and then every 2.5cm (1in) down the stripe to the opposite end. For the larger, more widely spaced crosses, place the first one 6.5cm (2½in) from the top raw edge and then every 5cm (2in).

The entire design is worked using three strands of wool. For the larger cross, first work a long straight stitch vertically down the cream stripe, before working the cross. Bring the yellow wool through to the right side of the fabric approximately 1.5cm (½in) above the marked dot, then insert the needle the same distance below the dot. Bring the needle out diagonally to the left (see illustration 1, below). Take the wool up towards the right side of the stripe,

*FAR RIGHT: Begin each cross with a vertical straight stitch down the centre of the cream stripes, before taking the needle out diagonally towards the left, ready for the next stitch.*

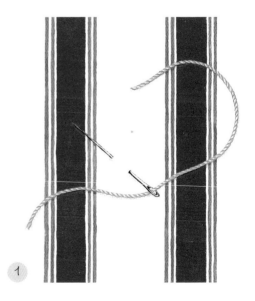

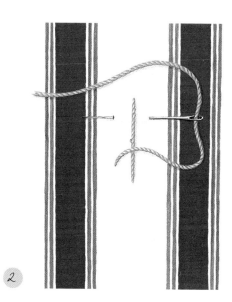

2

crossing over the centre of the straight stitch, and insert the needle. Pass the needle to the left of the stripe (see illustration 2, above). To complete the cross, take a diagonal stitch to the bottom right. Keep the stitches symmetrical, and remember that the cross should be slightly shorter in length than the first straight stitch (see photograph, page 81). Finally, finish each cross with a small straight stitch in plum red worked horizontally across all the yellow threads to secure them into position.

To work the smaller crosses, work as for the larger cross but omit the first straight stitch. Finish with a small straight stitch to secure the threads, but this time place it vertically over the cross.

### To make up the cushion cover

For the backing fabric you will need to mark and cut out two pieces of matching fabric, one measuring 53 x 63cm (21 x 25in) and the other 15 x 63cm

(6 x 25in). (These measurements include a 2.5cm/1in seam allowance all round.) To complete the cushion cover and to add piping, if desired, see page 126 for full instructions.

### To work the lampshade

Using a set square and a ruler, mark out a rectangle measuring 25 x 39cm (10 x 15½in) – the larger measurement is the circumference of the shade; the extra fabric is for making up and ease of sewing. Please note that I chose to place my stripes horizontally around the lampshade. Make sure that the stripes are arranged symmetrically, i.e., if you start with a cream stripe at the top of the shade, you must finish with a cream stripe at the bottom.

With a ruler and a washable fabric marker pen, mark out the position of the crosses as follows: Place the larger crosses 4cm (1½in) apart and the smaller crosses 1.5cm (½in) apart. Be very careful to keep the back of the work as neat as possible; any loose threads will show through the shade clearly when the lamp is turned on.

The entire design is worked with three strands of wool. Because the fabric I used for the lampshade has narrower stripes than the fabric I used for the cushion, the stitches are reduced in scale and the crosses extend to both sides of each stripe (see photograph, page 81). The stitching is exactly the same as for the cushion cover.

### To make up the lampshade

Add a 2.5cm (1in) seam allowance all round the lampshade outline, then cut it out. Make up the lampshade, referring to page 127.

*FAR LEFT: Cross the second straight stitch diagonally over the first stitch and bring the needle out again on the opposite side of the stripe.*

COLOUR GUIDE

**Yellow**
**8325**      **Plum red**
             **8106**

**Green**
**8305**      **Madder red**
             **8221**

# mystic symbols

*In tribal and folk art, a pattern engraved on a door or woven into a fabric is not merely decorative: it will also have one or more symbolic meanings, however abstract the pattern. Much of this meaning has now been lost to us, although the patterns are a constant source of inspiration. I have stitched rows of simple geometric motifs taken from early African pots onto a cushion cover of raw unbleached linen and a hemp table runner. The earthy colours are very much in keeping with the source of the inspiration.*

## MATERIALS

*For the cushion cover*
- DMC crewel wool in the following colours:
    - yellow 8484 (two skeins)
    - rust 8104 (two skeins)
    - maroon 8106 (two skeins)
    - plum 8123 (one skein)
- 1m (1yd) of 115cm (45in) wide (or wider) unbleached linen (or less if not piping)
- 48cm (19in) zip
- 2m (2¼yd) of piping cord (optional)
- 46cm (18in) square cushion pad

*For the table runner*
- DMC crewel wool in the following colours:
    - wine red 8212
    - deep red 8126
    
    (The amount of wool depends on the length of fabric to be embroidered. For my border, which measured 34cm/13½in, one skein of each colour was sufficient.)

- coloured linen or hemp table runner, or enough linen or hemp fabric made up as required

*For both projects*
- dressmaker's carbon paper
- embroidery hoop
- crewel (embroidery) needle size 4–6
- tracing paper

TEMPLATES

1

2

3

## STITCHES USED

chain stitch

laced running stitch (table runner only)

For full details on stitches, see pages 128–37.

## TECHNIQUES

For full information, see Techniques on pages 123–7.

## To work the cushion cover

Using a set square and a ruler, mark out a rectangle, 47 x 52cm (18½ x 20½in). To help position the pattern in straight lines, mark seven guidelines (see page 124) on the fabric – the lines of the pattern run parallel to the longest edge. Place the first line 5cm (2in) from one edge and the following six lines 7cm (2¼in) apart. The last line should be 5cm (2in) from the opposite edge. Add a 2.5cm (1in) seam allowance all round and cut out.

Trace the three templates with tracing paper and transfer the pattern onto the fabric with dressmaker's carbon paper. To position each template correctly, make sure that the centre of each one (as indicated by the dotted line) is positioned along a guideline. Starting on the left, arrange the pattern as follows: Place design 1 on the first guideline, 5.5cm (2¼in) from the top edge of the cushion, and repeat down to the bottom edge. On the second guideline, place design 2, and on the third guideline, place design 3. Repeat these three pattern lines once more and then finish with a third row of design 1 (see photograph, page 85).

The entire design is worked with three strands of wool in chain stitch.

Apart from the middle line, which is stitched in plum, design 1 is worked in maroon, design 2 in yellow and design 3 in rust. Embroider all the straight and curved lines with two rows of chain stitch. For the circles of design 1, first work an outer row of chain stitch (see illustration, right) before working an inner circle. The circles for designs 2 and 3 are worked in one continuous line of stitches, starting from the outside and spiralling in towards the centre.

## To make up the cushion cover

When the embroidery is complete, remove any tacking stitches. With a set square and ruler, mark and cut out two pieces of matching backing fabric, one piece 42 x 57cm (16½ x 22½in) and the other 15 x 57cm (6 x 22½in). (These measurements include a 2.5cm/1in seam allowance all round.) To finish off and to add piping, if desired, see page 126.

## To work the table runner

First mark a guideline (see page 124) 6cm (2½in) in from the hemmed edge. Mark out two more lines, 4cm (1½in) on either side of this first line. Trace design 3 with the tracing paper. Using dressmaker's carbon paper, transfer the template onto your border. For my narrow table runner, I repeated the complete design three times across the border; the narrowness of the fabric made it quite easy to calculate a

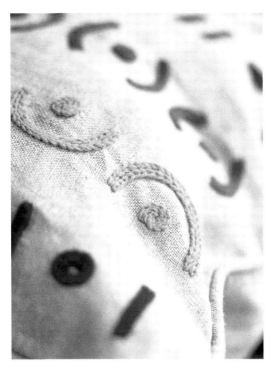

symmetrical arrangement. For a much longer border, place the first motif in the centre of the border and repeat the motif on either side of this central motif, making sure that the distance between each one is kept even. Work out towards both sides of the cloth; this means that the border pattern finishes symmetrically at the runner edges.

The entire design is worked with three strands of wool. Stitch exactly as for the cushion cover. The circles are embroidered in wine red and the curved lines in deep red. For the two outer lines, work single rows of running stitch in deep red and then lace them with the wine red wool.

When the embroidery is complete, remove any tacking stitches.

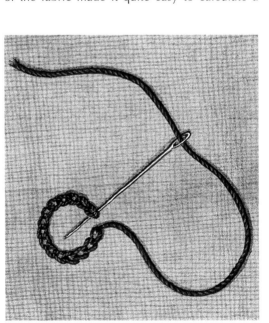

*FAR LEFT: To make a continuous line of chain stitch, link the last stitch of the embroidered line to the first. Slip the needle under the first stitch without penetrating the fabric. Draw the thread through and put the needle in again just next to the point where the thread emerged. Bring it up alongside the first stitch, ready to start the second, inner line.*

frippery

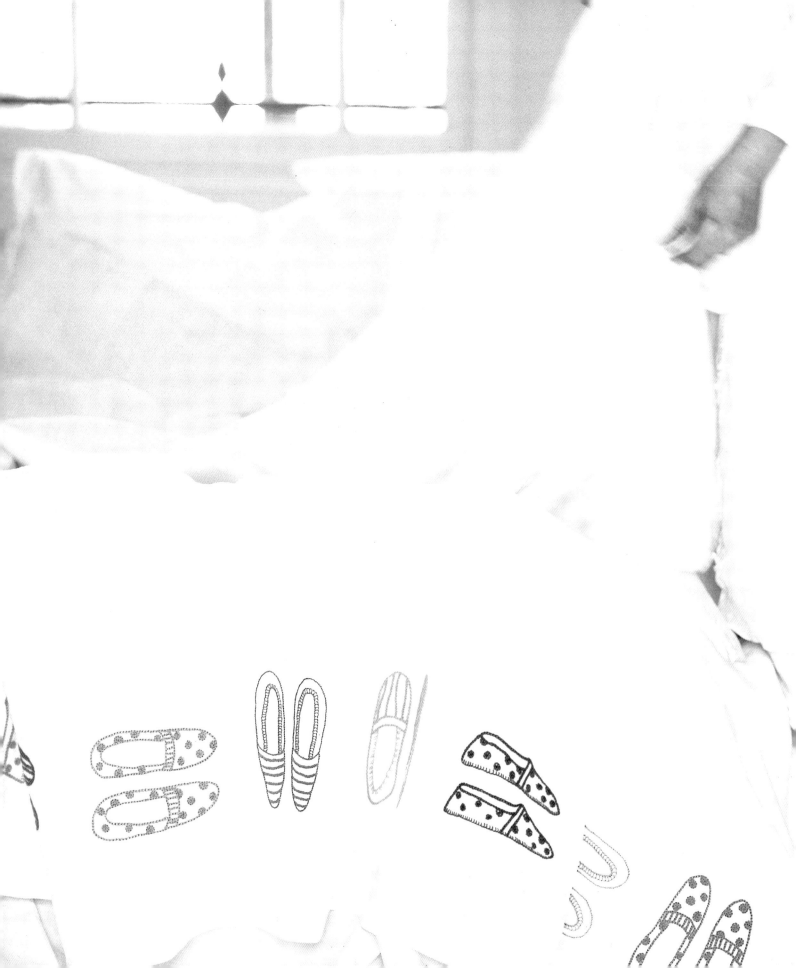

# this chapter is inspired by childhood memories – a pair of striped slippers, Granny's beaded evening bag, prettily iced birthday cakes, or Chinese paper lanterns hung across the playroom in a blaze of colour.

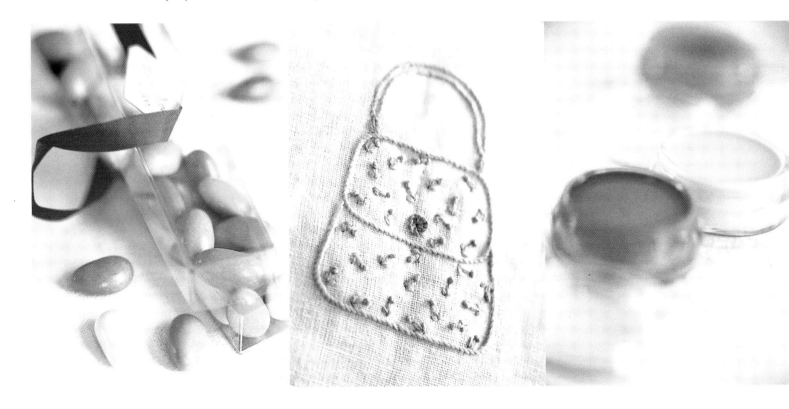

Images and colours were drawn from all these memories, and a few more, and edited into fresh and simple designs, full of fun and wit. Pairs of brightly coloured slippers dance across a bed cover, navy socks tip-toe along a linen shelf border, and a cushion frames an exquisite floral bag as if it were displayed in an exclusive shop window.

# hats

*A line of blue and white panama hats is stitched onto a hatband made from old blue and white mattress ticking. Their style and shape are a direct copy of the very hat they trim. Each hat is rather dainty, embroidered with two of the simplest stitches: running and stem. In addition, I added a line of panamas, although this time larger and bolder, onto a cream linen throw. I used chain stitch for the outline instead of the more delicate stem stitch, and to finish I sewed a length of wavy navy braid above the panamas to give added emphasis to the decorative border.*

## MATERIALS

*For the throw*
- DMC crewel wool in the following colours:
  slate blue 8207
  navy 8200
  (Quantities for the throw depend on the length of the border to be embroidered. One skein of both colours was sufficient for nine hats.)
- cream wool or linen throw, or if you prefer to make your own, sufficient fabric made up as required
- navy braid of sufficient length to decorate the border (optional)
- tracing paper

*For the hatband*
- DMC crewel wool in dark blue 8205 (one skein)
- 5cm (2in) width of striped cotton fabric (ticking is ideal) – the length depends on the size of the hat

*For both projects*
- dressmaker's carbon paper
- embroidery hoop
- crewel (embroidery) needle size 5–7

## STITCHES USED

  chain stitch (throw only)
  stem stitch
  running stitch
For full details on the stitches featured, see pages 128–37.

## TECHNIQUES

For full practical information on the methods used to make this project, refer to Techniques on pages 123–7.

### To work the throw

Trace the hat template with the tracing paper. Using a tape measure and sewing pins, plan the placement

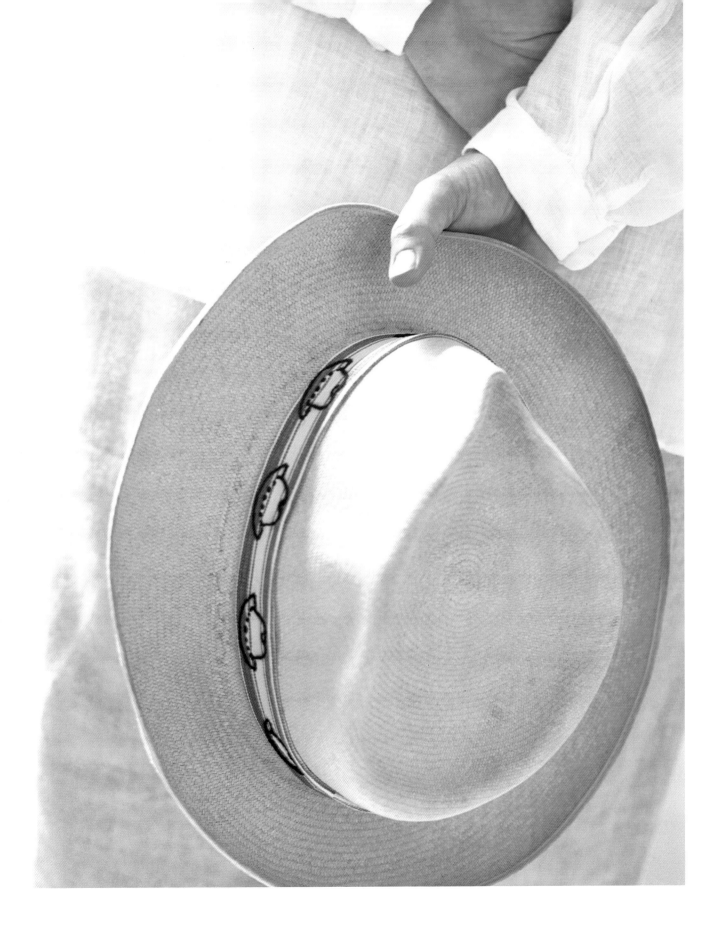

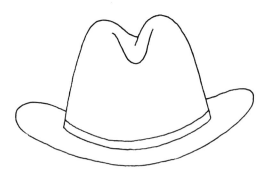

of the motifs so that they are evenly spaced along the border. To help you position the hats so that all their bases are level, you may want to mark a guideline (see page 124 for detailed instructions) – this should be 3cm (1¼in) in from the hemmed edge of the throw. Transfer the hat template onto the border with dressmaker's carbon paper, and use the guideline to ensure that the hats sit in a straight line.

With three strands of slate blue wool, outline each hat in chain stitch; with the same colour wool, but this time with just two strands, embroider a line of stem stitch for the dent of the hat. Change to three strands of navy wool and embroider three evenly spaced rows of running stitch to create the hatband, two along the marked lines on the template and one running in between. Work the two outline rows first, pairing the stitches, then work the middle row so that the stitches fall where the gaps are in the other rows. The overall effect should be staggered, like a woven fabric (see photograph, right).

For additional decoration, I chose to sew on navy braid above the line of hats. I positioned mine 7cm (2¼in) above the hat brims.

**To work the hatband**

Mark out a 5cm (2in) wide piece of fabric, long enough to fit round the crown of the hat. It is better not to cut out the strip until the embroidery is complete, as any excess fabric is useful for mounting the fabric into a hoop during sewing. Reduce the hat template to 54% and transfer it onto the fabric strip using dressmaker's carbon paper. Starting in the centre, arrange the hats in a level line along the hatband, approximately 2.5cm (1in) apart.

The entire design is worked with two strands of dark blue wool, except for the hat dent which is embroidered with one strand. Work the outline and the dent of the hat in stem stitch. Work two rows of running stitch for the hatband, one row directly below the other, pairing the stitches.

**To make up the hatband**

Add 1.5cm (⅝in) at each end of the embroidered fabric to allow for the seam allowance, then cut out. Sew the ends right sides together and press the seam. Fold under a 1cm (⅜in) hem along the top and bottom edges of the hatband. Press.

## COLOUR GUIDE

Slate blue
8207

Navy
8200

Dark blue
8205

*frippery* ● 95

# slippers

*Pairs of striped and spotted slippers, embroidered in a line but turning this way and that, decorate the top edge of a linen bed cover. The slightly irregular shape of each slipper is deliberate; I wanted the motifs to have a 'drawn by hand' feel, so they would look as though they had been outlined by a child. In addition, I chose the bright colours because of their association with childhood – beach balls, jars of jelly beans and wrapped sweets, for example. To complement the bed cover, I embroidered a pair of spotted slippers onto the front of a large draw-string bag; this reminds me of my first shoe bag.*

## MATERIALS

*For the bed cover*
- DMC crewel wool in the following colours:
    blue 8997
    green 8341
    yellow 8725
    orange 8129

(One skein of each is enough to embroider one pair of slippers.)
- plain cotton or linen bed cover or, if you prefer to make your own, sufficient fabric made up as required

*For the shoe bag*
- DMC crewel wool in the following colours:
    pinky red 8817 (one skein)
    green 8341 (one skein)
    bright pink 8153 (one skein)
- 55cm (22in) of 90cm (36in) wide (or wider) cream linen or cotton fabric
- 90cm (36in) of cord or ribbon
- tracing paper

*For both projects*
- dressmaker's carbon paper
- embroidery hoop
- crewel (embroidery) needle size 5–7

## STITCHES USED

Pekinese stitch          chain stitch

blanket stitch          stem stitch

eyelet buttonhole stitch

For full details on stitches, see pages 128–37.

## TECHNIQUES

For full practical information on the methods used to make this project, refer to Techniques on pages 123–7.

## To work the bed cover

Enlarge the four different slipper templates to 177% on a photocopier. It is a good idea to make several copies of each template so that you can plan the whole layout before transferring any of the pattern. Using a tape measure and sewing pins, plan the placement of the motifs along the border of the bed cover. To help position the slippers in a straight line, mark a guideline (see page 124 for detailed instructions) 17cm (6¾in) from the hemmed edge of the cover. Place the pairs of slippers evenly along the border, with the guideline passing directly through the middle of each pair. To prevent the design from looking too formal and regular, alter the direction in which the slippers point (see photograph, page 96). Transfer the slippers onto the fabric using dressmaker's carbon paper.

Although the choice of slipper style and the direction in which the slippers point along the bed cover border are random, the colours are used in a regular, repeating order. I started at one end of the cover with a pair of orange slippers, followed by green, blue and yellow. This colour sequence was then repeated to the other end of the cover.

The entire design is worked using two strands of crewel wool.

## SLIPPER 1

Work Pekinese stitch for the six stripes across the front of the slipper. Outline the slipper and the top of the slipper front in stem stitch. To embroider the inner pattern line, first work a row of blanket stitch, then a row of stem stitch.

## SLIPPER 2

Work Pekinese stitch for the four stripes running down the front of the slipper. Then work the outer edge of the slipper and the two lines across the front of the slipper in chain stitch. Now embroider the inner pattern line in blanket stitch, pairing the stitches (see illustration, left).

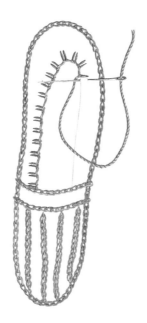

*RIGHT: For Slipper 2, embroider the inner pattern line in blanket stitch, pairing the stitches.*

TEMPLATES

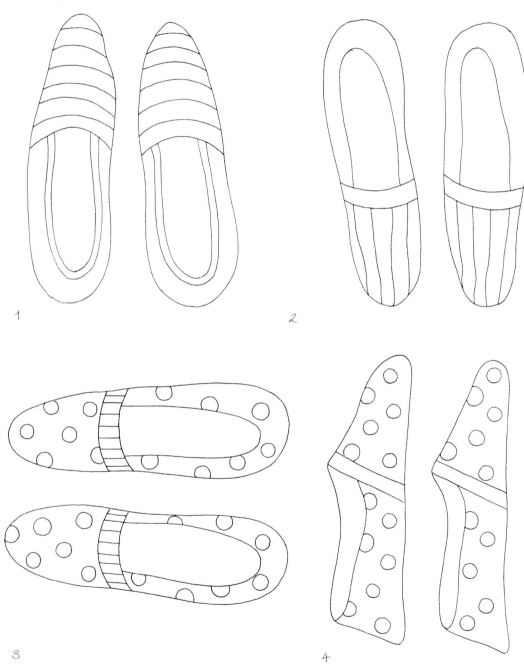

1

2

3

4

## SLIPPER 3

The entire slipper is worked in chain stitch. First embroider the striped band across the top of the front of the slipper, working the shorter lines (i.e., the lines facing the toe) before completing the two longer lines that cross the slipper from side to side. This will cover the ends of the shorter lines, giving a neat finish. For the circles, work one continuous line of chain stitch, starting from the outside and spiralling in towards the centre. Stitch the outline.

## SLIPPER 4

First work the sole of the slipper in blanket stitch and then complete all the circles in eyelet buttonhole stitch. Embroider the remaining lines in chain stitch.

### To work the shoe bag

Enlarge the template for Slipper 4 to 177% on a photocopier. Using tracing paper, reverse one of the slippers so that the soles of both slippers face each other (i.e., as a mirror image).

Cut the cream fabric in half so you have two pieces, each measuring 40 x 55cm (16 x 22in). Put one piece aside for the backing of the bag. Using dressmaker's carbon paper, transfer the template onto the other piece of fabric. (The longer measurement is the length of the bag.) Place the slippers 2cm (¾in) apart and 12.5cm (5in) from the bottom edge.

The entire design is worked with three strands of wool. Referring to the photograph (see left) for the use of colour, start by stitching the spots in eyelet buttonhole stitch, using the three colours randomly. Work the soles of the slippers in blanket stitch and then complete the remaining lines in chain stitch.

### To make up the bag

With the right sides of the fabric facing, sew the embroidered piece to its backing along the side and lower edges with 2cm (¾in) seams, leaving a 5cm (2in) opening on one side for the cord, approximately 12.5cm (5in) from the top. Turn under a 2cm (¾in) hem on the top edge. Turn the bag to the right side and fold over the top to the inside so that the fold line falls midway along the cord opening. Make a channel for the cord by stitching 2.5cm (1in) in from the top edge of the bag. The line of stitching will pass just under the opening for the cord. Use a safety pin to help thread the cord through the channel, then knot the ends together.

### COLOUR GUIDE

**Orange 8129**      **Yellow 8725**

**Green 8341**      **Blue 8997**

**Pinky red 8817**      **Bright pink 8153**

# gloves

Whether they are embroidered on a small scale as a repeating pattern along the edge of a cushion cover, or as a pair on the pockets of a gardening apron, these gloves are appealing because of their simplicity and naivety. To give the design a light touch, I chose to embroider it with a single outline of chain stitch and with just enough detail to suggest a zig-zag edging pattern, along with a few lines around the wrist of the glove. A versatile design, these gloves are discreet when small and stitched in subtle colours; large and embroidered in strong colours, they are witty and fun.

## MATERIALS

*For the cushion cover*

- DMC crewel wool in cream – ecru (two skeins)
- 30cm (12in) of 145cm (54in) wide unbleached linen fabric
- 58cm (23in) of 90cm (36in) wide cream linen
- a 50cm (20in) square cushion pad covered in cream linen or complementary fabric
- tracing paper

*For the apron*

- DMC crewel wool in green 8415 (two skeins)

- 60cm (24in) of 115cm (45in) wide (or wider) green linen fabric
- 32 x 46cm (12½ x 18in) rectangle of linen fabric in a contrasting colour for the pocket. (Alternatively, you may wish to use a ready-made apron.)

*For both projects*
- dressmaker's carbon paper
- embroidery hoop
- crewel (embroidery) needle size 5–7

## STITCHES USED

*For the cushion cover*

    chain stitch        back stitch

*FAR RIGHT: Working from right to left, embroider the decorative zig-zag border on each glove in back stitch.*

*For the apron*

    chain stitch        stem stitch

    running stitch

For full details on stitches, see pages 128–37.

## TECHNIQUES

For full practical information on methods used in this project, refer to Techniques on pages 123–7.

### To work the cushion cover

Using a set square and a ruler, mark and cut out from the unbleached linen two rectangles, each measuring 58 x 23cm (23 x 9in). (These measurements include a 2.5cm/1in seam allowance.) Put one piece aside for the backing.

Trace one of the glove templates using the tracing paper. To help place the gloves in a straight line, mark a guideline (see page 124 for detailed instructions) 6.5cm (2½in) in from one of the long edges. Use pins and a tape measure to plan the even spacing of the five gloves. Place the first glove 5.5cm (2¼in) from the side edge of the fabric and then each of the following gloves 2cm (¾in) apart, measuring from the tip of one glove to the base of the next. Transfer the motifs onto the border with dressmaker's carbon paper so that the centre of each glove is positioned on the guideline.

The entire design is worked with two strands of crewel wool. Outline each glove and work the decorative lines on the wrist all in chain stitch. Embroider the zig-zag trim at the base of each glove in back stitch (see illustration, below).

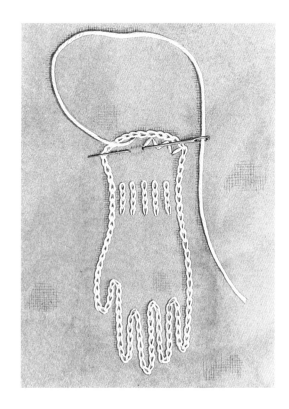

**To make up the cushion cover**

Cut the cream linen fabric in half to make two rectangles, each one measuring 58 x 45cm (23 x 18in). Take one rectangle and machine stitch it to the embroidered border, taking in a 2.5cm (1in) seam allowance (the right sides must be facing and the long sides aligning; for the embroidered piece, make sure that you join the long edge closest to the gloves to the fabric). Join the other two rectangles to form the back of the cover. Press both seams open.

With right sides facing, sew the front and back pieces together along the side and lower edges with a 2.5cm (1in) seam, leaving the border edge open. Turn under a 1cm (⅜in) hem on both sides of this edge. Turn the cushion cover to the right side and fold over 8cm (3¼in) of fabric to the inside all round to make a facing on the border edge.

To make ties for the cushion cover, cut the remaining unbleached linen into four strips, each measuring 28 x 7cm (11 x 3in). Fold each strip in half lengthwise, with right sides facing together. Machine stitch along the long side and one end, taking 1cm (⅜in) seams. With the blunt end of a pencil, turn each tube right side out. Press. Pin and tack the open ends of the ties into position inside the cushion cover, each one beginning 12.5cm (5in) from the side edge. Machine stitch two rows round the top edge to secure the ties and the facing. Work one row as near as possible to the open edge and the second 1.5cm (⅝in) in from the edge.

## To work the apron

Enlarge both gloves to 207% on a photocopier. Using dressmaker's carbon paper, transfer the pair of gloves onto the pocket fabric. Place each glove 11.5cm (4½in) from a side edge, i.e., the shorter edge, of the rectangle.

The entire design is worked with three strands of crewel wool.

Outline the gloves with chain stitch. Embroider the lines at the wrist of the glove and the decorative detail at the base in stem stitch.

## To make up the apron

Using a set square and a ruler, mark and cut out two rectangles of the green linen: 63 x 59cm (25 x 23in) for the skirt and 32 x 36cm (12½ x 14in) for the bib. (These measurements include seam and hem allowances; for both pieces the first measurement relates to the length.) Turn under a 2.5cm (1in) hem along the top edge of the pocket and a 1.5cm (⅝in) hem on the three remaining edges. Press.

Position the embroidered pocket centrally on the front of the skirt piece, 20cm (8in) from the bottom raw edge. Pin and tack, then, using three strands of green crewel wool, secure the pocket along the side and lower edges with a row of running stitches, making sure that the stitches are evenly spaced and of equal length. Sew a line of cream stitching down the centre of the pocket to make it into two. At the top of each line of stitching, oversew a few times to reinforce the pocket.

Turn under double 1.5cm (⅝in) hems along the side and lower edges of the apron skirt and the side and top edges of the bib. With right sides facing, pin

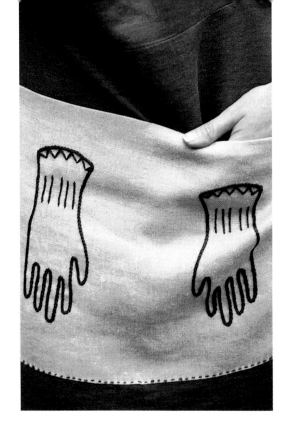

the bottom edge of the bib to the top of the apron skirt, making sure that it is placed in the centre. Sew the pieces together with a 2.5cm (1in) seam. Fold over the top of the apron, where it extends on either side of the bib, by the same amount, and machine stitch along the top of each side. Trim and press both the seam and hem.

To make the apron ties and the loop that goes around the neck, cut two strips of fabric, each measuring 60 x 6cm (24 x 2⅜in) and a third strip, 56 x 6cm (22 x 2⅜in). Fold each strip in half length-wise, wrong sides together. Tuck in the raw edges by 1cm (⅜in) all round, then machine stitch along all the edges.

Sew the two longer ties firmly onto the apron skirt, positioning one at each top corner, and the third onto the bib to form the neck loop. It is best to pin the loop in position first and then try the apron on; the tie can then be adjusted, if necessary, before being stitched in place.

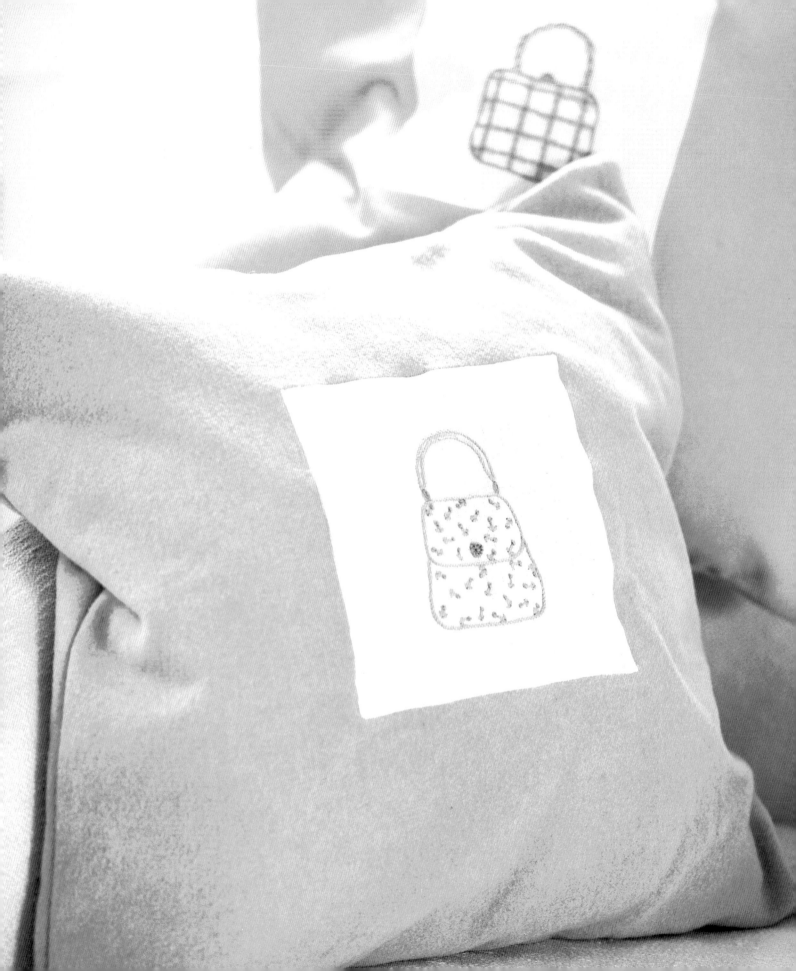

# handbags

*Appliquéd onto the front of two cushions made of the softest wool fabric are two lady-like handbags – one floral, the other 'beaded' in a grid pattern. On the former, the tiny flowers, resembling pretty sprigged cottons, are scattered randomly over the bag. Each flower is daintily embroidered in French knots and straight stitches. On the latter, in contrast, the 'beads' are arranged in a grid, with lazy daisy stitch creating the pattern. Each bag is clasped shut with eyelet buttonhole stitch.*

### MATERIALS

*For the cushion covers*
- DMC crewel wool in the following colours:
    - pink 8224
    - green 8420
    - beige 8505
    - pale yellow 8314 (for floral bag only)
    - golden yellow 8313 (for grid bag only)
    - (One skein of each is enough for two cushions.)
- 60cm (24in) of 115cm (45in) wide (or wider) wool fabric – blanket material is ideal
- 46cm (18in) zip
- 50cm (20in) cushion pad

*For the shopping bag*
- DMC crewel wool in the following colours:
    - pink 8224 (one skein)
    - green 8420 (one skein)
    - beige 8505 (one skein)
    - pale yellow 8314 (for floral bag only – one skein)

    - golden yellow 8313 (for grid bag only – one skein)
- 50cm (20in) of 90cm (36in) wide (or wider) heavy duty cream fabric – canvas or thick twills are ideal
- 60cm (24in) of thick cord or rope for handles

TEMPLATE

*For both projects*

- a 25cm (10in) square of cream cotton or linen fabric for each handbag. (Extra fabric has been included all round to allow for seams and for using the embroidery hoop.)
- dressmaker's carbon paper
- embroidery hoop
- crewel (embroidery) needle size 5–7

## STITCHES USED

| | |
|---|---|
| stem stitch | straight stitch |
| French knot | lazy daisy stitch |
| running stitch | eyelet buttonhole stitch |

For full details on stitches, see pages 128–37.

## TECHNIQUES

For full practical information on methods used in this project, refer to Techniques on pages 123–7.

TEMPLATE

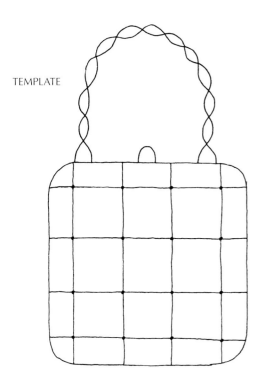

## GRID HANDBAG

Using beige, outline the body of the bag in stem stitch. To outline the handle, first work stem stitch in green in a continuous wavy line (see illustration, below) from one end to the other, then turn and work back towards where you started. At the points where the second line crosses the first, simply stitch over the top of the first line. Work the grid pattern of the bag in lazy daisy stitch and pink wool (see illustration, page 112). Then, in the centre of each group of lazy daisy stitches embroider one French knot in golden yellow. Finally, work a semi-circle of eyelet buttonhole stitch in green for the bag clasp.

**To work the cushion covers**

Enlarge the handbag of your choice to 123% on a photocopier. Using dressmaker's carbon paper, transfer the design onto a square of cream fabric, being careful to place it centrally.

The entire design is worked using three strands of crewel wool. Embroider the handbag of your choice as follows:

## FLORAL HANDBAG

Using pale yellow wool, outline the body and the handle of the bag in stem stitch. For each flower stem and pair of leaves, work three straight stitches in green. Complete each flower with a pink French knot for the flower head. Using beige wool, embroider a circle of eyelet buttonhole stitches for the clasp of the handbag and one lazy daisy stitch for each handle attachment.

1

*LEFT: The handle of the grid handbag consists of just two wavy lines worked in stem stitch. At the point where the second line crosses the first, simply stitch over the top of the first line.*

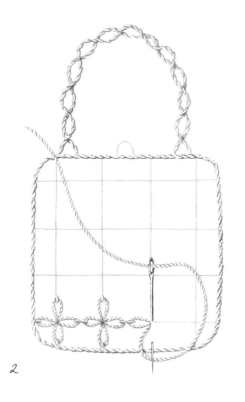

*RIGHT: Work the grid pattern of the grid bag in lazy daisy stitch. These are arranged in groups of four, with the centre of each group positioned at the point where the grid lines cross. The length of each stitch should not exceed more than half the height or width of each square.*

2

## To make up the cushion cover

Mark out around the embroidered handbag an 18cm (7in) square, making sure the motif is placed centrally within the square. Cut out.

Using a set square and a ruler, mark out on the wool fabric the following pieces: a 55cm (22in) square for the cushion front and two rectangles – one measuring 45 x 55cm (18 x 22in) and the other 15 x 55cm (6 x 22in) – for the back of the cushion. (These measurements include a 2.5cm/1in seam allowance.) Cut out.

Position the embroidered square on the right side of the front piece, making sure that it is exactly in the centre. Pin and tack. Secure in place by over locking the raw edges with a machine. Alternatively, if you prefer to hand stitch into place, turn under the raw edges before sewing.

Refer to page 126 for full instructions on how to complete the cushion.

## To work the shopping bag

Embroider the handbag of your choice, following the instructions given for the cushion. When it is complete, mark out an 18cm (7in) square round the embroidered handbag and cut out. Turn under a 1cm (⅜in) hem all round and press.

## To make up the shopping bag

With a set square and ruler, mark out on paper a rectangle measuring 46 x 36cm (18½ x 14in) – this includes a seam allowance and makes a squared-off version of the final bag. Cut out your rectangle and fold it in half lengthwise. Draw a freehand curve along one of the corners away from the fold. When you are happy with the shape, cut it out and unfold the paper to give you the full bag shape with its two curved bottom corners. Use this template to mark out two bag shapes on the heavy duty fabric.

Pin and tack the embroidery on the front of one piece, 13cm (5in) from the lower edge. Using three strands of the golden yellow thread, secure all round with a row of running stitches, making sure the stitches are evenly spaced and equal in length.

With right sides facing, sew the back and front pieces together along the side and lower edges with 2cm (¼in) seams. Turn under a double 2.5cm (1in) hem on the top edge. Turn the bag to the right side.

On the remaining fabric, mark and cut out two strips measuring 7.5 x 33cm (3 x 13in). Fold them in half and machine stitch along the two long sides to make two tubes. Turn to the right side and insert 30cm (12in) of thick cord or rope. Hand sew the ends of each handle onto the inside of the bag, firmly encasing the cord.

## COLOUR GUIDE

**Pink**
**8224**

**Green**
**8420**

**Beige**
**8505**

**Pale yellow**
**8314**

**Golden yellow**
**8313**

# bedtime

*I drew inspiration for this project from the brightly coloured paper outfits I used to cut out for dressing small dolls made of cardboard. Traditional blue- and white-striped pyjamas are stitched across a purple pyjama case, looking like a line of dolls assembled ready for bed, and matching socks decorate the border of a cupboard shelf. The pyjamas are all identically stitched – stem stitch for the outlines and stripes, and French knots for the buttons – while the socks are embroidered in three different ways, with some areas in solid chain stitch.*

## MATERIALS

*For the shelf border*

- DMC crewel wool in the following colours:
    navy 8205 (two skeins)
    purple 8333 (two skeins)
- plain cream linen or cotton fabric (see under 'To work the shelf border' for quantity)

*For the pyjama case*

- DMC crewel wool in the following colours:
    navy 8205 (two skeins)

cream – ecru (two skeins)

- 1m (1yd) of 90cm (36in) wide (or wider) coloured linen fabric
- three buttons
- tracing paper

*For both projects*
- dressmaker's carbon paper
- embroidery hoop
- crewel (embroidery) needle size 5–7

## STITCHES USED

*For the shelf border*

| | |
|---|---|
| chain stitch | stem stitch |
| Pekinese stitch | running stitch |

*For the pyjama case*

| | |
|---|---|
| stem stitch | French knot |

For full details on stitches, see pages 128–37.

## TECHNIQUES

For full practical information on methods used in this project, refer to Techniques on pages 123–7.

### To work the shelf border

Measure out a strip of fabric to the length and width of your shelf, adding 10cm (4in) to the width for the embroidered border and a further 2.5cm (1in) all round for the hem allowance. Cut out.

Enlarge the socks to 110% on a photocopier. With a tape measure and pins, plan the placement of the socks. To help position them so that their bases are all level, mark a guideline (see page 124) 4cm (1½in) from the unhemmed edge of the fabric. Transfer the motifs onto the border with dressmaker's carbon paper, using the guideline as placement for the dotted template line.

The entire design is worked with two strands of crewel wool. Sock 1 is worked in the same way

TEMPLATES

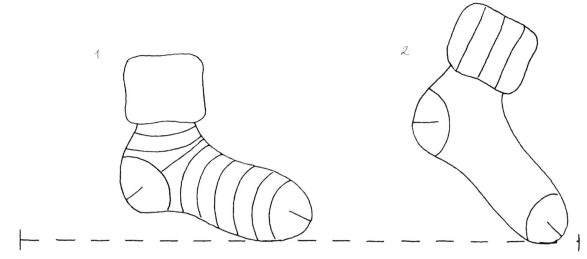

throughout the border, while sock 2 is worked in two different ways (see photograph, page 115). Embroider each sock as follows:

## SOCK 1

Embroider the top of the sock in solid chain stitch using navy, working in horizontal lines (see illustration, below). Work a line of chain stitch on either side of this coloured area, making sure that the stitches cover the ends of each horizontal line. This will give you a neater finish as well as helping to define the shape of the sock. Outline the rest of the sock and the toe and heel area in stem stitch. Change to purple thread and work all the remaining pattern lines in chain stitch.

## SOCK 2 – VARIATION A

Using navy and working in chain stitch, embroider the heel and toe in solid colour, then outline the whole of the sock, including the turn-over. Change to purple wool and embroider the three decorative lines marked on the top of the sock in Pekinese stitch; then on either side of these lines work rows of running stitch. Over the solid-coloured toe and heel area work 'gusset' lines of chain stitch (see illustration, below).

## SOCK 2 – VARIATION B

Using purple wool and working in chain stitch, embroider the three decorative lines marked on the top of the sock, the outline of the turn-over and the two lines for the toe and heel detail. Change to navy wool and work the outline of the sock, including the toe and heel, in chain stitch. On either side of the three decorative lines at the top of the sock, work rows of running stitch.

When the embroidery is complete, remove any tacking stitches. Hand sew a hem all round.

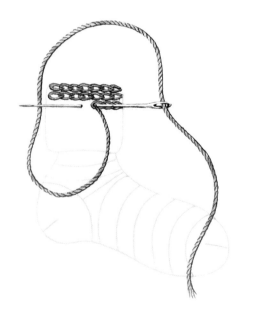

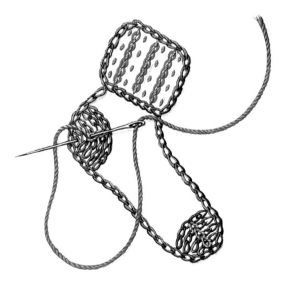

*FAR LEFT: To create solid lines of colour for the top of Sock 1, work horizontal rows of chain stitch. Place the rows close together so no fabric is visible.*

*LEFT: For both the heel and toe of Sock 2 (variation A), embroider a 'gusset' line in chain stitch directly over the solid navy stitching. Work from the inside out towards the sock outline, finishing just within the outline.*

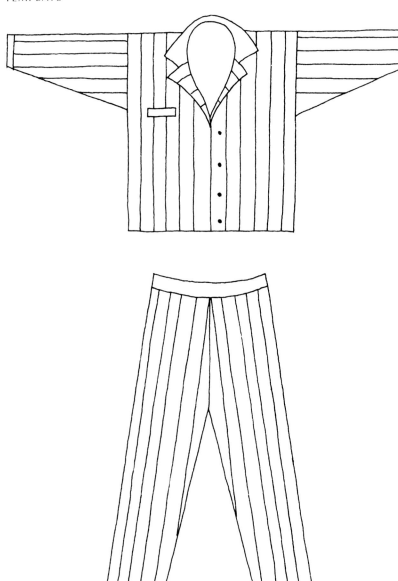

## To work the pyjama case

With a set square and a ruler, mark out the following pieces of fabric: 33 x 50cm (13 x 20in) for the pyjama bottoms, 30 x 50cm (12 x 20in) for the pyjama tops and 41 x 50cm (16 x 20in) for the backing. All these measurements include a seam allowance. Put the backing to one side.

Trace the pyjama template using the tracing paper and make three copies. Transfer the motifs onto the fabric with dressmaker's carbon paper. Place the pyjama tops 13cm (5in) in from the bottom edge of the fabric, measuring from the base of each top. Position the first pyjama top in the centre of the fabric and then the other two on either side at a distance of 2.5cm (1in), measuring from one sleeve edge to the next. Place the pyjama bottoms 13cm (5in) in from the top edge of the fabric, measuring from the top of each motif. Position each pyjama bottom so that it will lie directly below a corresponding pyjama top.

The entire design is worked with two strands of wool. Except for the pyjama buttons, the only stitch used is stem stitch. Ignoring all outlines and dividing lines, as well as pockets and waistbands, work each alternate stripe in navy (see photograph, pages 114–15). Embroider all the remaining lines in cream. Fill the top of the collar with several lines of stem stitch, following the curve of the collar. For each button on the front of the pyjamas, embroider a cream French knot.

## To make up the pyjama case

On the pyjama bottom piece, turn under a 2.5cm (1in) hem to the wrong side on the top edge.

Machine or hand stitch in place. Repeat this for the pyjama top piece, then turn under a further 7.5cm (3in) to the wrong side to form a facing, and pin it in position. Place this piece so it overlaps the bottom piece and the distance between the base of the pyjama tops and their corresponding bottoms is 4cm (1½in). This will make a flap. Pin these two pieces together to secure them temporarily.

With right sides facing, pin the front of the pyjama case to the backing. Stitch a 2.5cm (1in) seam all round. Press the seams and flap, then turn the case to the right side. Sew on the buttons, positioning each one just above each pyjama bottom. The flap will slightly overlap each button. Make a fine button loop with the navy wool along the edge of the top piece to correspond with each button.

## COLOUR GUIDE

**Navy**
**8205**

**Purple**
**8333**

**Cream**

**ecru**

# techniques & stitches

## FABRICS FOR EMBROIDERY

Almost any fabric can be used for embroidery with wool, from near-transparent materials, such as lawn and muslin, to denim and heavy linens, and even felt and woollen blankets. A design with fine outlines and delicate details is more effective on a fabric that has a smooth surface and is closely woven. On the other hand, a bolder design using thicker wool requires a coarser and more loosely woven fabric.

Linen has always been the favourite fabric for embroidery with wool, and it is what I have used for most of the projects in this book. A hardwearing fabric, which comes in a range of different thicknesses, textures and colours, it allows the needle and wool to pass smoothly and easily through it without distorting either the material or the design. Whichever fabric you choose, make sure that it is an even-weave fabric – this means it has an equal number of threads (warp and weft) in each direction. The evenness of weave allows the stitches to be kept in perfect alignment.

## EMBROIDERY THREADS

Just as almost any fabric can be used for embroidery, so, too, can most threads, from silks, cottons and linens to wools – even twine. The choice depends largely on the type of embroidery and how you intend to use it. The same stitch can produce varied effects with different types of thread. For

those pieces that will be washed frequently, for example an embroidered tablecloth or hand towel, the design should be stitched using a cotton thread that launders well, with no distortion of the design. For more decorative pieces that require little washing or dry cleaning, for example a curtain or a throw, wool thread can be used.

Crewel wool is the most popular wool embroidery thread. A fine, twisted 2-ply yarn, it can be used singly or stranded together, as required. Persian yarn, also 2-ply, is popular, too, but differs from crewel wool in that it comes with three strands loosely bundled together, which can then be separated. Tapestry wool is thicker than

crewel wool, which makes it ideal for bolder designs on heavier fabrics (see the Reflecting Swirls throw, page 26, for example). Also suitable is fine knitting wool, particularly 2-ply botany wool, which I sometimes use instead of tapestry wool. Although all the threads I have mentioned are widely available in an excellent selection of colours, I have chosen to use crewel wool for the majority of the projects in this book because of its versatility.

When buying wool for these projects, please note that the amounts given are only rough guides: how much you use will depend on how closely together you work the stitches, how much thread you use in starting and finishing, and the tension of your stitching. If you wish to reproduce my crewel designs exactly, you will need to buy the same colour, brand and weight of wool thread that is given for each project. A conversion chart is provided on page 143, should you wish to substitute threads of another brand.

Embroidery wools are usually packaged in hanks or skeins. Some are wound so that the lengths can be pulled out easily, as in Persian yarn, while others, such as crewel wool, need the skein band removed and the yarn untwisted before it can be used. If you wish, these skeins can be cut at each end to create a bundle of threads the right length for stitching. If you knot the bundle loosely in the centre, it will not tangle.

## NEEDLES

Different types of embroidery require different types of needle, and it is important to choose the right one. The crewel needle – about 4.5cm (1 ¾in) in length, with a long, slender eye and a sharp point to pierce the fabric easily – is the most commonly used. These needles are numbered 1 to 10; the higher the number, the finer the needle. The eye of the needle must be large enough to allow the thread to pass through smoothly without fraying but, in turn, the threaded needle must not be too thick to pass through the fabric. If a needle leaves a large hole in the fabric, choose a finer one. For thicker wools that cannot be threaded through a crewel needle, or when embroidering twill or blanket fleece, use a chenille needle. These are identical to tapestry needles except that they have a sharp point. The oval-shaped eye is large enough to allow thick yarns to be threaded.

When buying needles, choose packs of mixed sizes to allow for experimentation. In time, all needles will start to lose their shiny plating, appear tarnished and feel sticky. They should then be replaced.

## FRAMES

A round wooden frame or embroidery hoop with a screw adjustment is a useful, if not essential, tool for most embroidery. The smaller (inside) ring is placed under the fabric at the point where you wish to stitch; the larger ring is then placed over the top and the screw tightened until the fabric is held tautly and evenly. This keeps the fabric smooth and the stitches flat while you are working. The hoop should always be removed when you have finished stitching; if left in place, it can stretch and mark the fabric. For large pieces of embroidery, where a design is too big to fit into the area of even the largest hoop available, the hoop can be moved around.

Frames are available in a range of sizes and shapes, and I would suggest that you visit your local needlework shop to seek advice on which to use. For some embroidery, a frame is not essential, particularly if you are using very simple stitches on thicker fabrics. There are no strict guidelines for using frames: some people like to use one for all their embroidery, while others prefer to work the fabric in the hand. What is important is that everyone should work in the way they feel most comfortable.

## ADDITIONAL EQUIPMENT

Apart from needles and frames, few other tools are required for successful embroidery. A large pair of scissors is essential for cutting fabric, as is a pair of small, very sharp pointed embroidery scissors. Dressmaker's carbon or transfer paper is needed for transferring patterns onto fabric (see right, Transferring the pattern). The latter is a non-smudge carbon paper, available in several colours; always choose a colour that contrasts well with your fabric, so that the working lines will be clearly visible.

A water-soluble marking pen is ideal for drawing details directly onto the fabric, while tracing paper is essential if you are transferring designs directly from this book onto the fabric, without enlarging or reducing them. Finally, and perhaps the most important of all is a good light source.

## DRAWING A GUIDELINE

To ensure that you stitch in a straight line, you may find it helpful to draw a guideline on your fabric. For this, you can use either tailor's chalk or a water-soluble marking pen on the reverse of the fabric. Then tack along the line to form a stitched guideline on the right side of the fabric.

## TRANSFERRING THE PATTERN

Once you have decided on the design you wish to embroider and have assembled your materials, you will need to transfer the design onto the fabric. Each project in this book includes a template or line drawing of the design. For some projects, the templates are the actual size, and you simply have to trace the pattern with tracing paper; once traced, it can then be transferred (see right). Other templates have been scaled down to fit into the book, and so these will need to be enlarged to the correct or desired size. This is very easily done on a photocopier, and the percentages of enlargement are given with each project, where required. For large, all-over, non-repeating designs that need enlarging quite substantially (see the Jacobean Blooms template, page 40), you will have to copy and enlarge the template in parts, unless you have access to an extra-large photocopier. To do this, photocopy the template once, then divide the design into four equal parts using a ruler and pen. Enlarge all the parts to the required size, trim any excess paper, then tape the pieces together to create a whole template. Make sure you match the pattern lines carefully.

For projects with a repeating pattern, it is a good idea to make several copies of the template. During the transferring process, a copy can become worn out, even torn, through constant redrawing.

The simplest way to transfer a design onto fabric is to use dressmaker's carbon paper; this is the method I have used for all my designs. The whole design must be transferred before you start stitching. This is particularly important for repeating patterns, which require careful placement. (Once stitching has started, it is very difficult to line up a pattern successfully.)

Before transferring the design, you need to press the fabric so that it is completely smooth. Then, place the fabric right side up on a flat, hard surface, holding it in position with masking tape, if necessary. Place the carbon paper, shiny side down, on the fabric, securing it with tape, then place the traced or photocopied design on top of this and tape down to secure. Trace carefully over the design with a fine ballpoint pen, pressing hard to produce carbon lines that can be seen easily and will not brush off before the embroidery is complete. Avoid leaning on the carbon paper, as it does have a tendency to smudge. When the tracing is complete, carefully remove both the carbon and pattern papers. On smooth fabrics, such as linen, a design will transfer easily, giving you good, clear lines. On softer, fleecy fabrics, such as woollen blankets, try not to press too hard with the ballpoint pen as it may sink through both the pattern and carbon papers, thus marking the fabric with ink. Mark the fabric gently (turn up one corner to see whether the design has transferred, even faintly), and then redraw the design firmly with a water-soluble marking-pen so it is absolutely clear on the fabric.

Sometimes a design can be drawn directly onto the fabric, thus by-passing the need for carbon paper. A water-soluble pen is ideal for this. Do not use a pencil as the lead will dirty the fabric as well as the wool.

## STARTING AND FINISHING WORK

Where you start your stitching is a matter of personal preference. I prefer to begin with the outline of a motif and then move on to fill in the centre. It is always better to work in a continuous flow, rather than starting in several different places; in this way the embroidery design will join up successfully.

An embroidery thread should be cut in lengths of no more than 50cm (20in); any longer and they are likely to twist and knot and be difficult to work with. The neatest way to start stitching is to make a few tiny running stitches towards your starting point and then make a small back stitch. These stitches should be worked in the area or along the line to be embroidered so that they will be hidden by subsequent decorative stitches. Where these small starting stitches will not be covered by embroidery, for example, when working French knots, either run the thread under a few existing stitches at the back before starting, or leave a 5cm (2in) loose thread at the back of the fabric and catch it down with the first few stitches. Always avoid making knots.

When working your embroidery, try to make sure that the stitches cover the carbon paper lines fully, so that no carbon shows through when the stitching is complete. When finishing, the thread should be woven through the back of the last few stitches. Once the thread has been secured in this way, the excess can be cut off.

Once finished, the embroidery must be pressed. If it is soiled or there are still traces of carbon, and all the materials used are washable, wash gently in cool water with wool detergent (the wool thread will shrink in hot water); otherwise dry-clean.

Embroidery worked with cotton threads rather than with wool can be washed in hot water. To avoid flattening the stitches during pressing, place a thick towel or an old sheet, folded several times, over the ironing board and place the embroidery face down on top. Cover with a damp cloth and press until dry.

## MAKING UP A CUSHION

Making up a cushion is a simple process and if you do not have a sewing machine, hand stitching is just as effective. Although zips are optional, they do allow the cushion pad to be removed easily. Alternatively, you can leave a gap at the bottom of a cushion, stitching it up after the cushion pad has been inserted. For this type of closure you will need to cut just one piece of fabric for the cushion back, to the same size as the front piece. If, however, you choose to use a zip, you will need to cut two pieces of fabric for the cushion back. The sizes of these pieces depend on the size of the embroidery, and all the correct measurements are given with the working instructions for each project.

With right sides facing, pin the two back pieces together. Stitch at each end of the central seam, leaving enough seam open in the middle for the length of the zip fastener. Pin and tack the zip fastener into position and stitch with a sewing machine with a zip foot or by hand using back stitch. If you want to add piping, see below before proceeding any further.

With right sides facing (the zip open, if you are using one), pin and then stitch the embroidered front to the backing. If you are not fitting a zip fastener, you will need to leave a gap in one of the seams just big enough to insert the cushion pad. Trim any excess fabric and clip the corners diagonally to minimize bulk. Turn the cushion cover right side out, press the seams and insert the cushion pad. If a gap has been left, oversew it neatly to close.

## PIPING

Piping is made from fabric cut on the bias (i.e., diagonally) and wrapped around piping cord. The fabric used can be either the same as the cushion itself or contrasting. Piping cord is available in a range of thicknesses; choose fine cord for a delicate trim and a thicker cord for a more prominent effect.

Cut the fabric into strips on the bias, wide enough to wrap around the cord and to allow 1cm (⅜in) on each edge for seam allowances (see illustration 1, above right). Join the strips to form the required length, right sides together, and stitch together (see illustration 2, below right). Press the seams. Wrap the binding round the cord, wrong sides facing, and stitch as close to the cord as possible using a zip or piping foot on the sewing machine. Place the covered piping on the right side of the embroidered front piece, with the raw edges together, so that the piping lies set in from the fabric edge.

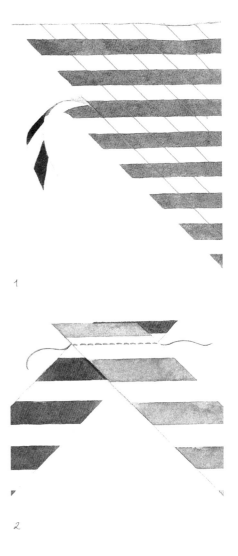

1

2

Clip the seam allowance on the piping to ease the fit on the corners. To join the two piping ends, fold back the fabric and trim the cord ends so that they meet end to end. Unfold the fabric so that it covers the abutted ends; turn under a 5mm (¼in) hem on one of the strips, and stitch over the join.

Place the backing fabric over the piping and pin all three layers together, then stitch as close as you can to the piping, taking particular care at the corners. Finally, trim the seams following the instructions given on page 126 for cushions.

## LAMPSHADES

### To make a pattern

Lay a sheet of paper on a flat surface and secure it in position with masking tape. Place an existing lampshade (or frame) in one corner of the paper, starting at one strut, and roll it across the paper in an arc until the first strut makes contact with the paper

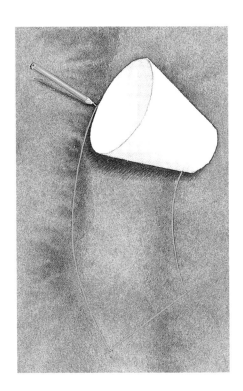

again (see illustration, below left). As you roll the shade (or frame) slowly across the paper, mark the top and bottom arcs with a pencil. Cut out the paper pattern. This is the pattern for your lampshade.

### To cover an existing lampshade

The following is the simplest way to cover a lampshade with embroidery; the result is just as effective as making your own shade from scratch, but a lot easier.

Choose a ready-made (i.e., covered) lampshade of the required size; the lighter the colour and the thinner the cover, the better. It is very important that the cover is made of a smooth material and not textured.

Lightly spray the outside of the shade with adhesive so that it is evenly coated. Wait a minute or two for the glue to become tacky, then place the embroidered fabric over the shade and smooth it into position. The spray glue allows for repositioning if you do not manage to get it in the right place the first time. Where the fabric ends overlap, fold the top end under to make a neat edge and then glue this down to hide the raw edge of the other end. With your hand, smooth out any wrinkles in the cover, pushing them to either edge. When the fabric is completely smooth, fold the excess at the top and bottom edges over to the inside of the shade and glue into position. Use clothes pegs to secure the turn-overs in position while the glue is drying.

To trim the shade and to hide the raw edges, run fabric adhesive along one side of the cotton tape and attach it to the bottom of the shade, beginning at the join and folding it over to the inside as you go. Where the ends met, turn under one of the raw edges and stick it down so that it neatly overlaps the other raw edge. Repeat for the top of the shade. If you do not wish to have any trimming visible on the outside of the shade, apply the tape to the inside of the shade only, making sure it covers all the raw edges of the embroidered fabric.

# stitches

### ALGERIAN EYE

One of the most delightful ways of grouping single stitches is with Algerian eye stitch: eight straight stitches radiate out from a central point to form an eye or star. It is important to keep the stitches symmetrical, otherwise much of their charm is lost. Work on the straight of the fabric, following a fabric thread to line up each stitch evenly.

### BACK STITCH

This discreet needlework stitch can also be very decorative when worked in embroidery threads and wools. Depending on the thread or material used, the stitches may be larger than those used in ordinary sewing. If the stitches are kept very small, back stitch can outline any shape, which makes it ideal for fine lines, curves, tiny stems and tendrils.

### BLANKET STITCH

Although blanket stitch is most frequently used as a decorative finishing edge on a blanket, it can be as effective in a decorative design. It is perfect for thorny or spiky edges, for outlining simple shapes and as a filling stitch when worked in rows interspersed with lines of stem stitch. It should not be confused with buttonhole stitch.

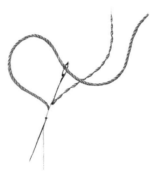

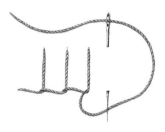

### To work

The classic blanket stitch is worked between two parallel lines using stitches of equal length. Working from left to right, bring the wool through on the bottom line and hold it down below the line with the left thumb. Insert the needle to the right on the top line and bring it out on the bottom line directly below, with the point of the needle over the held wool, i.e., the loop. Pull the needle through until the wool lies flat on the material with the loop pulled tight, but not so tight that the fabric puckers. Continue working in this way. For curved edges, the stitches are graduated to follow the curve (see Paisley Curls, page 12).

### To work

Bring the wool through where the centre of the eye will be and make one straight stitch horizontally to the left. Bring the needle up in the centre again and make a horizontal stitch, this time to the right. Work two more straight stitches in this way vertically, making sure they form perfect right angles to the first two stitches. Then divide each right angle evenly in half with four diagonal stitches to complete the eye.

### To work

Working from right to left, bring the needle up through to the right side of the fabric and make a short backward stitch along the working line. With the needle now at the back of the work, take a long stitch forward and bring the needle up to the left of the first back stitch. This long stitch should be twice the length of the back stitch. Take another short back stitch to the right, inserting the needle where the first back stitch began; this ensures that there are no gaps between the stitches to create a neat solid line. Make sure that all the stitches are of even length.

## CHAIN STITCH

Chain stitch is made up of single looped stitches which are linked together to form a line or chain. Its simplicity and neatness make it an excellent stitch for outlining areas as well as for filling shapes (see Trailing Flowers, page 54). Crewel embroidery from India is usually worked entirely in chain stitch, while in Jacobean patterns it is frequently used for shading.

### To work

Bring the needle through where the first stitch is to start and hold down the wool towards you with the left thumb. Put the needle in to the right of where the wool first emerged and take a downward stitch along the working line. Pass the wool under the point of the needle from left to right and draw through the needle until the loop lies flat. Hold down the wool and insert the needle just to the right of the emerging wool and inside the loop already made. Work a stitch of the same length as the previous one. Hold the last loop in place with a small vertical stitch.

## CABLE CHAIN STITCH

Cable chain stitch is slightly more intricate than chain stitch, but still not difficult. While chain stitch is formed by passing the wool under the needle point, for cable chain stitch the wool is twisted into a loop around the needle before the stitch is made. It is useful for border patterns and bold designs (see Reflecting Swirls, page 26).

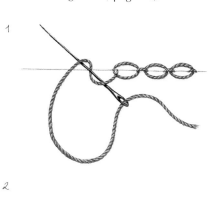

### To work

**1.** Working from right to left along a single line, bring the needle up at your starting point and pull the wool through. With the needle in your right hand, hold the wool along the line with your left and wrap the wool once around the needle.

**2.** Keeping the loop of wool taut around the needle, insert it into the material a little distance from where the wool first emerged, and make a short stitch along the line. Pull the working wool until the loop is tight around the needle, then, keeping the wool under the point, draw the needle through towards the left to complete the chain stitch. Continue in this way to the end of the line and secure the last stitch with a long tacking stitch. For best results, keep the stitches even.

## COUCHING STITCH

When a thread is laid on top of the fabric and caught down at intervals by small stitches in a separate yarn, this is known as couching. The holding-down stitch is usually embroidered in a colour that contrasts with that of the thread being held down, unless the design calls for an unbroken line. There are many ways in which the threads can be held in place. The holding-down stitch can be made in either very simple stitches, such as straight and satin stitches, or more decorative stitches like herringbone and buttonhole stitches. For the projects in this book, I have used couching in its simplest form (see Coral Lines, page 18), and with just one variation, a decorative cross stitch (see Wispy Tendrils, page 58).

distance from the beginning of the line and just below the wool to be couched down. Insert the needle above this wool to make a small vertical stitch to hold it in place, then bring the needle through to the right side again a little further along the line in position for the next stitch. Continue in this way, keeping the stitches even and making sure the thicker wool lies smooth on the fabric. A common mistake to make is to pull the wool taut and wrinkle the material.

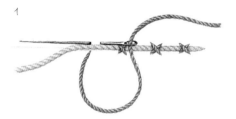

working cross stitch, particularly on a fine fabric where the woven threads cannot be counted, it helps to imagine that you are placing the cross stitch inside a square box, with the threads crossing diagonally from corner to corner.) Next insert the needle diagonally to the right at the top of this wool and then bring it out again to the left directly above where the first stitch emerged, but still keeping the needle above the wool to be couched.
**2.** Take the wool down to the lower right-hand corner to complete the cross, and bring the point of the needle out again where you wish the next cross stitch to be. All the stitches should cross in the same direction.

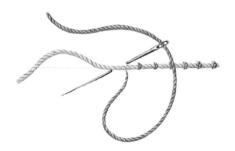

### To work simple couching
Bring the wool that is to be couched down through to the right side of the fabric and lay it along the line to be worked. Thread another needle with a finer wool of matching or contrasting colour and bring it through a short

### To work cross stitch couching
**1.** Bring the wool to be stitched down through the fabric as for simple couching. Thread another needle with a finer wool and bring it through a short distance from the beginning of the line and just below the wool to be couched down. (When

## DOUBLE CROSS STITCH

Also known as star stitch, double cross stitch consists of a straight cross embroidered over a regular cross stitch. Although the stitch is simple to make, its success depends on the regularity of the stitches. The slant and length of each stitch must be even. If you are worried about doing this stitch freehand, mark the double cross first on the fabric. This is a useful and interesting stitch for filling a large area as well as for giving it texture. It can be arranged in rows or scattered for a powdery effect.

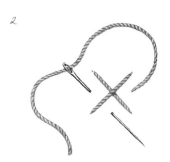

### To work

When working freehand, it helps to imagine that you are placing the cross inside a box, with the diagonal stitches passing from corner to corner and the straight lines crossing the centre at perfect right angles.

**1.** Bring the needle through to the right side of the fabric at the point that represents the bottom right-hand corner of the box, and work one diagonal stitch to the top left-hand corner. Point the needle vertically down and bring it out again to the right side at the bottom left-hand corner. Work a second diagonal stitch, this time to the right, so that it crosses the first stitch. Point the needle vertically down but this time bring it out again half-way between the two stitches and directly in line with the centre of the cross.

**2.** Work a straight stitch horizontally to the left, inserting the needle on the opposite side of the cross. Bring the needle through at the base of the cross between the two diagonal stitches and work a vertical stitch, crossing the horizontal stitch at a perfect right angle.

## EYELET BUTTONHOLE STITCH

Eyelet buttonhole is a very useful stitch for embroidering small flowers and flower centres as well as for decorative dots (see Slippers, page 97, and Noughts & Crosses, page 71).

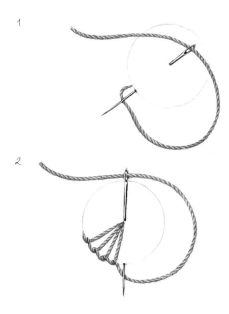

### To work

**1.** Working from left to right, bring the wool through to the right side of the fabric on the working line. Hold down with the left thumb and insert the needle in the centre of the circle. Bring the needle out on the working line just below, with the point of the needle over the held wool.

**2.** Pull the needle through until the wool lies flat with the loop pulled tight. Continue until the circle is filled. Always insert the needle into the same hole at the centre.

## FERN STITCH

This dainty stitch is useful for feathery leaves or stems as well as for leaf veins. It consists of just three single stitches of equal length worked from a central line.

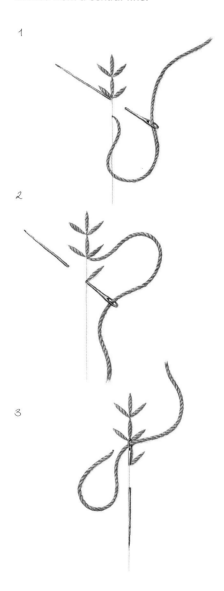

## To work

**1.** Working from top to bottom, bring the needle through one stitch length down the central working line. Work one single stitch to the right, at a 45-degree angle to the central line. Point the needle back towards the left, and bring it out at the top of the central line.

**2.** Make a stitch down the central line, inserting the needle at the bottom of the diagonal stitch, then make one single diagonal stitch to the left, similar in length and angle to the one on the right.

**3.** Pull the needle through and take it back to the central line, inserting it at the base of the first and second stitches. Take a stitch of the same length as the others down the central line, then repeat the three stitches for the required length.

## FLY STITCH

This versatile stitch can be used singly, scattered within a shape to form a light powdery filling; combined in groups for decorative effect; or in rows to make a border pattern.

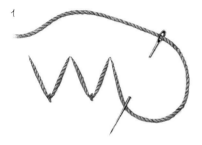

## To work

**1.** Working from left to right, bring the needle through where the top of the stitch is to be and hold the wool down towards you. Insert the needle to the right, in line with where the wool first emerged, and take a diagonal stitch downwards to the centre point. Pull the needle through, with the wool held under the point of the needle, to form a V shape.

**2.** Insert the needle just below the wool to make a tiny vertical holding stitch. Bring the point out at the top of the next stitch.

## FRENCH KNOT STITCH

This detached stitch consists of a single knot that lies on top of the fabric. The thickness of the wool determines its size. It is the perfect stitch for the centre of flowers (see Handbags, page 109).

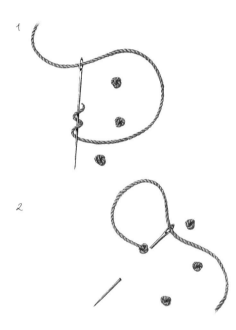

### To work

**1.** Bring the needle through to the right side. Hold the wool taut with the left hand and wind it round the needle twice.

**2.** Turn the needle round and, keeping the wool taut, insert it into the fabric close to where the wool first emerged. Pull the needle through gently, allowing the knot to slide down the needle until it is resting on the fabric. Release the wool at the very last minute to avoid making a sloppy knot.

## GUILLOCHE STITCH

Guilloche stitch is composed of three basic stitches – satin, lacing (or threading) and French knots. Like many composite stitches, second and third colours can be introduced for contrast. When complete, it forms a decorative band which is most effective used for borders (see Sea Waves, page 31).

### To work

**1.** Embroider groups of three horizontal satin stitches (see page 137) in a row across the fabric, with spaces and stitches of equal length.

**2.** Working from left to right in laced running stitch (see page 135), bring the contrasting wool up behind the first block of stitches, pulling it through at the top. Slide the needle under the second group from top to bottom, without piercing the fabric, and pull through. Slide the needle from the bottom to the top under the next group. Continue to lace the following blocks, alternately top to bottom, bottom to top, being careful not to pull the wool too tight.

**3.** At the end of the row, reverse direction and lace in the opposite manner back to the beginning to create a chain-like effect of circles linked with satin stitch.

**4.** Embroider a French knot (see left) in the centre of each circle.

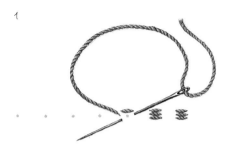

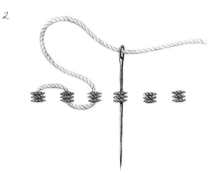

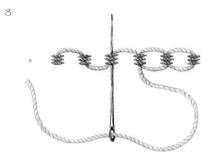

## LACED RUNNING STITCH

When a stitch is woven with a secondary thread, it is known as lacing. For single laced running stitch, the thread passes in and out of running stitch in one direction only. If it returns back again to the beginning, it is known as double laced running stitch and resembles chain stitch. It is important to use a blunt pointed tapestry needle for lacing to avoid piercing the base fabric. Lacing also offers the opportunity of introducing a second colour, thus creating a more decorative stitch.

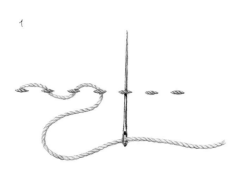

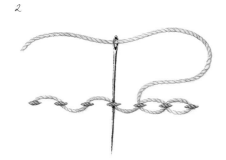

## To work

**1.** First embroider a row of running stitches (see page 136) along your working line. Bring the lacing thread up at the beginning of the row, just above the first running stitch. Slide the needle under the second stitch from top to bottom and then slide it back up again under the third stitch. Continue in this manner, weaving in and out of the running stitches, until you reach the end of the row. Take the needle through to the back of the work to finish off. Remember, lacing does not pierce the fabric except at the beginning and end of the row.

**2.** For double laced running stitch, follow the instructions for single lacing, but at the end of the row do not pull the wool to the back of the work; instead, lace back to the beginning of the row in the opposite direction, making sure the needle goes under both the running stitch and the first line of lacing.

## LAZY DAISY STITCH

Lazy daisy is also known as detached chain stitch because each stitch or chain link stands alone, secured at the top by a small holding stitch.

## To work

**1.** Bring the needle through at the top of the first stitch and hold the wool down towards you with the left thumb. Insert the needle just to the right of where the wool first emerged, then take a downward stitch of the required length. Pass the thread under the needle point from left to right. Draw the needle through until the wool lies flat.

**2.** Insert the needle just beneath the loop to make a vertical holding stitch. Bring it out again at the top of the next stitch.

## PEKINESE STITCH

This is another composite stitch in which a base row of stitching is laced with another thread, giving the opportunity to introduce a second colour. It is a stitch most frequently associated with Chinese embroidery, where it is used in row after row as shaded filling. For the projects in this book, I have used it to create bold decorative crosses (see Noughts & Crosses, page 71) as well as for fine detail (see Slippers, page 97).

### To work

**1.** First embroider a row of large, evenly spaced back stitch (see page 128) along your working line. Bring the second or contrasting thread up near the second stitch on the left-hand side. Pull through.
**2.** Slide the needle down under the first stitch and then slide it up again under the third stitch.
**3.** Go back to the second stitch and pass the needle down under both the stitch and the threading. Pull through. Continue in this way, being careful not to pull the thread too tightly. Do not allow the needle to pierce the fabric, except at the beginning and end of the lacing. It is best to use a blunt pointed tapestry needle for this. Once you get into the rhythm of the lacing, it is a very simple and quick stitch.

1

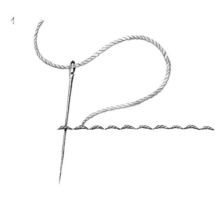

2

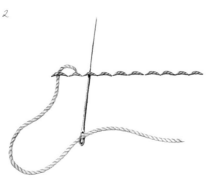

3

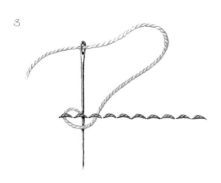

## RUNNING STITCH

This stitch is identical to the running stitch used in sewing but it has a very decorative feel when embroidered in crewel wool. It consists of short, even stitches that run in and out of the fabric in a straight line; the size of the stitches depends on the thickness of the embroidery thread used. It is a useful stitch for embroidering thin, curved lines (the sharper the curve, the smaller the stitches should be).

### To work

Working from right to left, pass the needle in and out of the fabric to create a broken line of stitches along the line to be worked. It is important to keep the stitches and the spaces between the stitches even. The resulting effect depends not only on the size of the stitches but also on the thickness of the wool used: the thicker the embroidery thread, the larger the stitch.

## SATIN STITCH

Satin stitch is the most commonly used stitch for filling an area with solid colour. The effect is achieved by working single stitches side by side so that no fabric shows through. Satin stitch is ideal for smaller shapes such as petals and leaves, but less suitable for larger areas of work, where the stitches tend to become loose and untidy.

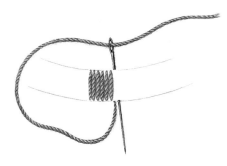

### To work

Bring the needle through to the right side at the bottom of the space to be filled, then insert it at the top edge and bring it out again at the bottom, close to where the first stitch emerged. Continue in this way, making parallel stitches, until the whole area is filled. The stitches can be upright or sloping, but the angle of the first stitch will determine the direction for all the others. Be careful not to overlap the stitches or to pull too tightly.

## STEM STITCH

This quick and easy stitch produces a solid line which makes it particularly good for outlining a design. When used as a filling, it is known as crewel stitch. Altering the angle of the stitches will vary the thickness of the line. Usually the needle is held at a slight angle and enters the fabric below the working line and comes out above it; if a narrower line is desired, the needle can pass directly along the working line.

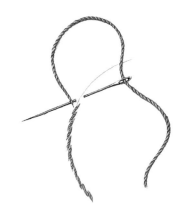

### To work

Working from left to right, bring the needle through to the right side, just to the left of the working line. Take the needle a little way along the line and, pointing it back to the left, insert it just to the right of the line, so that the stitch lies at a slight angle. Pull the needle through and repeat, keeping the length and angle of the stitches even. The stitches can be worked with the thread to the right or the left of the needle, as long as you are consistent.

## STRAIGHT STITCH

Straight stitch is a single, isolated flat or satin stitch, and forms the basis of many other stitches. It can vary in length and direction but should not be loose. The stitches can be grouped in many different ways to create simple shapes (see Stars & Stripes, page 80), or they can be set apart from any neighbouring stitch to add detail to a design.

### To work

Bring the needle through to the right side of the fabric and make one stitch of any length and in any direction. If several straight stitches are to be worked close together, make sure that you bring the needle out in the right place to start the next stitch.

# index

Entries with initial capital letters
are titles of embroidery projects.

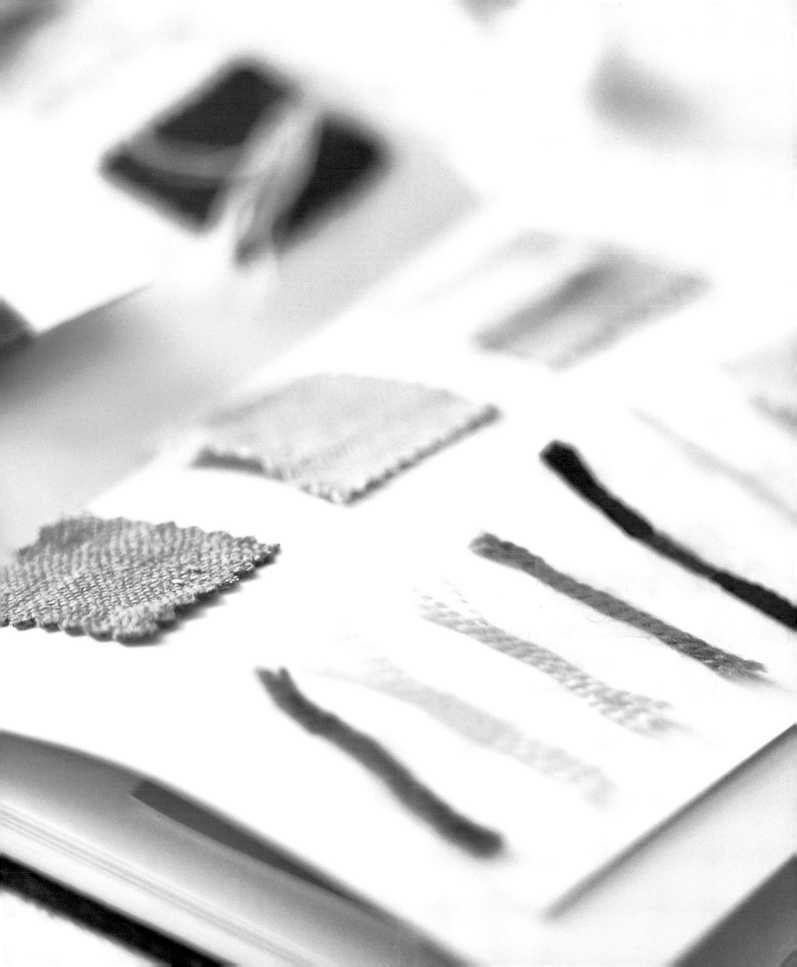

THE DESIGNS IN THIS BOOK were embroidered with DMC crewel wool and DMC tapestry wool. If you prefer to work in Appleton crewel and tapestry wools, refer to the conversion chart below, which lists all the DMC shades used, followed by the nearest equivalent Appleton shade. Please note that the Appleton shades may produce slightly different results from those shown in the photographs. Both DMC and Appleton wools are widely available in department stores and needlework shops. If you have problems finding a stockist near you, contact the relevant distributor listed below.

**DMC crewel wool – Appleton crewel wool**

| | | | | | | | |
|---|---|---|---|---|---|---|---|
| 8104 - 724 | 8127 - 447 | 8207 - 853 | 8224 - 753 | 8333 - 895 | 8484 - 695 | 8817 - 946 | 8997 - 564 |
| 8106 - 226 | 8129 - 624 | 8208 - 323 | 8305 - 311 | 8341 - 253 | 8505 - 182 | 8838 - 187 | ecru - 992 |
| 8111 - 751 | 8153 - 801 | 8209 - 321 | 8313 - 694 | 8401 - 253 | 8725 - 844 | 8896 - 451 | |
| 8123 - 606 | 8200 - 929 | 8212 - 148 | 8314 - 692 | 8415 - 646 | 8798 - 463 | 8908 - 994 | |
| 8126 - 504 | 8205 - 928 | 8221 - 723 | 8325 - 473 | 8420 - 251A | 8799 - 462 | 8932 - 321 | |

**DMC tapestry wool – Appleton tapestry wool**

| | | | | | |
|---|---|---|---|---|---|
| 7036 - 483 | 7108 - 995 | 7202 - 753 | 7423 - 902 | 7540 - 833 | ecru - 992 |

## Distributors

**DMC**

UK
DMC Creative World
Pullman Road
Wigston, Leicester
LE18 2DY
Tel: 0116 2811040
Fax: 0116 2813592

AUSTRALIA
DMC Needlecraft Pty Ltd
51-66 Carrington Road
Marrickville, NSW 2204
Tel: 02 559 3088
Fax: 02 559 5338

JAPAN
DMC K.K.
3-7-4-203 Kuramae
Taito-Ku
Tokyo 111
Tel: 3 582 84112
Fax: 3 582 84117

NEW ZEALAND
Warnaar Trading Co Ltd
376 Ferry Road
PO Box 19567
Christchurch
Tel: 03 89288
Fax: 03 3891823

SOUTH AFRICA
S.A.T.C.
43 Somerset Road
PO Box 3868
Capetown 8000
Tel: 2 141 980 40
Fax: 2 141 98047

**APPLETON**

UK
Appleton Bros Ltd
Thames Works
Church Street
London W4 2PE
Tel: 0181 994 0711
Fax: 0181 995 6609

AUSTRALIA
Stadia Handcrafts
PO Box 357
Beaconsfield
NSW 2014
Tel: 612 9565 4666
Fax: 612 9565 4464

JAPAN
Sanyei Imports
2-64 Hirakata
Fukuju-cho
Hashima-shi
Gifu

Tel: 058 398 5144
Fax: 0081 583 98 5132

NEW ZEALAND
Nancy's Embroidery Ltd
326 Tinakori Road
Thorndon
Wellington
Tel: 04 473 4047

SOUTH AFRICA
Needlepoint
PO Box 662
Northlands 2116
Johannesburg
Tel: 0027 11 447 1883
Fax: 0027 11 784 1947

# acknowledgments

**Author's**   I wish to thank everyone who helped me on this book, especially Helen Ridge, Alison Barclay and Suzannah Gough at Conran Octopus; Alison Bolus, Carolyn Jenkins, Suki Dhanda, Carrie Armstrong, Margie Swabey, Rachel and Kit, Dean Whitlock, Cara Ackerman at DMC, Fiona Lindsay, my agent; and Jane Moran and Tracey Seaward for the use of their wonderful homes.

Very special thanks go to Isobel Hunt, who stitched so beautifully and tirelessly with me, and to Sandra Lane, without whose wonderful eye and support this book would not have been the same.

Finally, a big thank you to Charles, as always, for his constant encouragement and unending support.

**Publisher's & Author's**   The publisher and author would like to thank the following: Kerstin Ever at Ever Trading, 12 Martindale, East Sheen, London SW14 7AL (0181 878 4050) for the fur throw used for the Spirals & Pinwheels project; Bryony Thomasson, 19 Ackmar Road, London SW6 4UP (0171 731 3693) and Sheila Cook, 42 Ledbury Road, London W11 2AB (0171 792 8001) for their generous loan of textiles for styling; and Richard Joseph Ward, Furniture Designer, 3 Ezra Street, London E2 7RH (0171 729 6768) for the use of his beautiful sofa for the Coral Lines project, and the rocking deck-chair for the Contemporary Circles project.